T0198953

MACAT

An Analysis of

David Graeber's

Debt

The First 5,000 Years

Sulaiman Hakemy

CONTENTS

WAYS IN TO THE TEXT

Who Is David Graeber?   9

What Does *Debt: The First 5,000 Years* Say?   10

Why Does *Debt: The First 5,000 Years*?   12

SECTION 1: INFLUENCES

Module 1: The Author and the Historical Context   15

Module 2: Academic Context   19

Module 3: The Problem   24

Module 4: The Author's Contribution   28

SECTION 2: IDEAS

Module 5: Main Ideas   32

Module 6: Secondary Ideas   37

Module 7: Achievement   42

Module 8: Place in the Author's Work   45

SECTION 3: IMPACT

Module 9: The First Responses   49

Module 10: The Evolving Debate   52

Module 11: Impact and Influence Today   56

Module 12: Where Next?   59

Glossary of Terms   64

People Mentioned in the Text   71

Works Cited   76

THE MACAT LIBRARY

The Macat Library is a series of unique academic explorations of seminal works in the humanities and social sciences – books and papers that have had a significant and widely recognised impact on their disciplines. It has been created to serve as much more than just a summary of what lies between the covers of a great book. It illuminates and explores the influences on, ideas of, and impact of that book. Our goal is to offer a learning resource that encourages critical thinking and fosters a better, deeper understanding of important ideas.

Each publication is divided into three Sections: Influences, Ideas, and Impact. Each Section has four Modules. These explore every important facet of the work, and the responses to it.

This Section-Module structure makes a Macat Library book easy to use, but it has another important feature. Because each Macat book is written to the same format, it is possible (and encouraged!) to cross-reference multiple Macat books along the same lines of inquiry or research. This allows the reader to open up interesting interdisciplinary pathways.

To further aid your reading, lists of glossary terms and people mentioned are included at the end of this book (these are indicated by an asterisk [*] throughout) – as well as a list of works cited.

Macat has worked with the University of Cambridge to identify the elements of critical thinking and understand the ways in which six different skills combine to enable effective thinking.
Three allow us to fully understand a problem; three more give us the tools to solve it. Together, these six skills make up the **PACIER** model of critical thinking. They are:

ANALYSIS – understanding how an argument is built
EVALUATION – exploring the strengths and weaknesses of an argument
INTERPRETATION – understanding issues of meaning

CREATIVE THINKING – coming up with new ideas and fresh connections
PROBLEM-SOLVING – producing strong solutions
REASONING – creating strong arguments

To find out more, visit **WWW.MACAT.COM.**

CRITICAL THINKING AND *DEBT: THE FIRST 5,000 YEARS*

Primary critical thinking skill: PROBLEM-SOLVING
Secondary critical thinking skill: REASONING

Debt is one of the great subjects of our day, and understanding the way that it not only fuels economic growth, but can also be used as a means of generating profit and exerting control, is central to grasping the way in which our society really works.

David Graeber's contribution to this debate is to apply his anthropologists' training to the understanding of a phenomenon often considered purely from an economic point of view. In this respect, the book can be considered a fine example of the critical thinking skill of problem-solving. Graeber's main aim is to undermine the dominant narrative, which sees debt as the natural – and broadly healthy – outcome of the development of a modern economic system. He marshals evidence that supports alternative possibilities, and suggests that the phenomenon of debt emerged not as a result of the introduction of money, but at precisely the same time.

This in turn allows Graeber to argue against the prevailing notion that economy and state are fundamentally separate entities. Rather, he says, "the two were born together and have always been intertwined" – with debt being a means of enforcing elite and state power. For Graeber, this evaluation of the evidence points to a strong potential solution: there should be more readiness to write off debt, and more public involvement in the debate over debt and its moral implications.

ABOUT THE AUTHOR OF THE ORIGINAL WORK

Born in 1961, US anthropologist and activist **David Graeber** was weaned on leftist politics, and declared himself an anarchist at age 16. He became an anthropology professor, and his early cultural research in Madagascar exposed him to poverty that he saw as caused by pressures to repay excessive government debt. Through a combination of activism and scholarship he has devoted much of his career to developing an intellectual basis for undermining capitalism. In his 2011 book Debt: The First 5,000 Years, Graeber uses the insights of an anthropologist to argue that debt plays a toxic role in human relations.

ABOUT THE AUTHORS OF THE ANALYSIS

Sulaiman Hakemy holds an MSc in economic history and development from the London School of Economics. A writer and journalist, he has reported on industry, politics, and culture for various publications. His background is in the development aid and urban planning sectors, specialising in conflict and fragile states. He is based in Istanbul and Toronto, and speaks English, French, Spanish, Arabic, Persian, and some Urdu.

ABOUT MACAT

GREAT WORKS FOR CRITICAL THINKING

Macat is focused on making the ideas of the world's great thinkers accessible and comprehensible to everybody, everywhere, in ways that promote the development of enhanced critical thinking skills.

It works with leading academics from the world's top universities to produce new analyses that focus on the ideas and the impact of the most influential works ever written across a wide variety of academic disciplines. Each of the works that sit at the heart of its growing library is an enduring example of great thinking. But by setting them in context – and looking at the influences that shaped their authors, as well as the responses they provoked – Macat encourages readers to look at these classics and game-changers with fresh eyes. Readers learn to think, engage and challenge their ideas, rather than simply accepting them.

'Macat offers an amazing first-of-its-kind tool for interdisciplinary learning and research. Its focus on works that transformed their disciplines and its rigorous approach, drawing on the world's leading experts and educational institutions, opens up a world-class education to anyone.'

Andreas Schleicher
Director for Education and Skills, Organisation for Economic Co-operation and Development

'Macat is taking on some of the major challenges in university education ... They have drawn together a strong team of active academics who are producing teaching materials that are novel in the breadth of their approach.'

Prof Lord Broers,
former Vice-Chancellor of the University of Cambridge

'The Macat vision is exceptionally exciting. It focuses upon new modes of learning which analyse and explain seminal texts which have profoundly influenced world thinking and so social and economic development. It promotes the kind of critical thinking which is essential for any society and economy.
This is the learning of the future.'

Rt Hon Charles Clarke, former UK Secretary of State for Education

'The Macat analyses provide immediate access to the critical conversation surrounding the books that have shaped their respective discipline, which will make them an invaluable resource to all of those, students and teachers, working in the field.'

Professor William Tronzo, University of California at San Diego

WAYS IN TO THE TEXT

KEY POINTS

- Born in 1961, David Graeber is an American professor of anthropology* (the study of human beings, particularly human culture, practices, and beliefs) and a social activist supporting anarchism* (the political position that there should be no government).

- In his 2011 book *Debt: The First 5,000 Years*, Graeber tells the story of debt in human history and argues that money, markets* (systems in which goods and services are bought and sold), and our current economic system were created to help the wealthy take advantage of the poor.

- *Debt* gives readers an alternative to the traditional understanding of economics.*

Who Is David Graeber?

David Graeber, the author of *Debt: The First 5,000 Years* (2011), is an anthropologist and professor of anthropology at the London School of Economics* in England. He has published many books on topics related to both anthropology and politics,* and has also been involved in international activist movements focused on anti-globalization* (opposition to the increasing economic, cultural, and political connectedness across continents), anti-capitalism* (opposition to the economic and social system of capitalism, in which trade, production, and property are held in private hands), and the support of debt relief.

Graeber was born in New York in 1961, where his parents exposed him to leftist politics at an early age. His mother was a garment worker and his father fought against the right-wing General Franco* in the Spanish Civil War* (1936–9). Both were active in labor union* politics (a union is an organization of traders, workers, or laborers who join together to negotiate for things such as better salaries or working conditions). While Graeber's father was associated with anarchist movements during his time in Spain, he never claimed to be an anarchist; David Graeber, however, began to consider himself an anarchist at the age of 16.

Graeber received his doctorate in anthropology from the University of Chicago in 1997. In graduate school, Graeber won a prestigious Fulbright Fellowship* to conduct ethnographic* fieldwork—the study of a people in the place where they live—on the island of Madagascar in the Indian Ocean. While there, he saw firsthand the devastating effects that large amounts of government debt can have on developing countries.*

Graeber has been active in protest movements for years. He served as an intellectual leader in the Occupy Wall Street* movement, which started in 2011 and opposes economic and social inequality. Graeber has been credited with coining the group's anti-inequality slogan "We are the 99%."1

What Does *Debt: The First 5,000 Years* Say?

David Graeber's 2011 book *Debt: The First 5,000 Years* asks whether our economic system and its morals are fair. As Graeber writes, "this book is a history of debt … but it also uses that history as a way to ask fundamental questions about what human beings and human society are or could be like."2 To do this, Debt takes a critical look at some of the founding "myths" of modern economics. It also offers different ways of thinking about economies, using the insights of anthropology.

Since the time of the influential Scottish economist Adam Smith* (1723–90), economics has been grounded on the idea that human relations are based on exchange: on trading one thing for another. Graeber says this makes it seem "as if our ties to society, even to the cosmos itself, can be imagined in the same terms as a business deal."[3] One of the central themes in the book is Graeber's argument that exchange is not the most fundamental thing about humanity.

Smith, who pioneered economics as a field of study, argued that money was created in ancient times to make barter* more convenient. In a moneyless barter system, something is traded directly for something else, so that two people can do business together only if each has something the other wants. Graeber argues that there is no evidence to show that money was created for this purpose. Smith also claims that the state and the free market—an economic system in which parties are free to buy and sell goods and services without government interference—are opposing forces. Graeber, on the other hand, says the two "were born together and have always been intertwined."[4]

Graeber says that "the very principle of exchange emerged largely as an effect of violence," and that money and markets find their origins "in crime and recompense, war and slavery, honor, debt, and redemption."[5] This is an important secondary theme in *Debt*.

At the same time, Graeber uses his background in anthropology, studying human society, beliefs, and practices, to discuss the "moral basis of economic life."[6] He suggests that human beings shift between different types of economic interaction with one another. Of these different types, "exchange," Graeber argues, usually occurs among strangers.

Graeber also describes differences between the market economy and the pre-market economy, which he calls the "human economy." Human economies are "economic systems primarily concerned not with the creation of wealth, but with the creation, destruction, and rearranging of human beings."[7] In these economies, money is not used to buy things, but rather to maintain relations between people. When states and empires introduced market systems, exchange became the chief form of interaction between people.

The final argument in *Debt* is that money and debt have historically alternated between virtual and physical forms. Graeber says this demonstrates that money, debt, and the system of capitalism*—in which trade, production, and property are in private hands—are not a fundamental part of human nature. They are social creations that can be undone.

Why Does *Debt: The First 5,000 Years* Matter?

Debt was first published in 2011, and written in a time of global economic turmoil, when many were already questioning the fairness of the dominant economic system. Two major economic crises together have demonstrated the devastating impact that excessive debt can have on quality of life. The global financial crisis of 2008* was caused in part by financial institutions lending many people far more money in home mortgages than they could possibly repay. The government response to the crisis focused on stabilizing the financial system by rescuing banks, rather than on providing debt relief for individuals. In the ongoing European debt crisis,* nations in southern Europe that have borrowed enormous amounts of money are being pressured to reduce their national budgets in favor of repaying loans to wealthier countries and institutions. These budget cuts have led to enormous political fallout by worsening the problems of widespread unemployment and poverty—issues that have led some to challenge their assumptions about justice and debt. Graeber's book provides a framework for thinking about these issues.

Graeber believes his arguments will only become more relevant over the coming years:"There is very good reason to believe that, in a generation or so, capitalism itself will no longer exist."[8] Graeber sees

Debt pointing the way toward this future reality. He urges readers to believe they can play a role in determining the future of the system: "What I have been trying to do in this book is not so much propose a vision of what, precisely, the next age will be like, but to throw open perspectives, enlarge our sense of possibilities; to begin to ask what it would mean to start thinking on a breadth and with a grandeur appropriate to the times."[9]

The author brings significant new insights into these economic issues by examining them through the lens of anthropology. While *Debt* makes no policy prescriptions other than simple debt relief, it quickly became a hit in international activist circles. Graeber has positioned himself as an influential voice in debates about not only debt, but about the kind of society we should aspire to live in.

NOTES

1   David Runciman, "*The Democracy Project: A History, a Crisis, a Movement* by David Graeber – Review," *Guardian*, March 28, 2013, http://www.theguardian.com/books/2013/mar/28/democracy-project-david-graeber-review.

2   David Graeber, *Debt: The First 5,000 Years* (Brooklyn, NY: Melville House, 2011), 18.

3   Graeber, *Debt*, 18.

4   Graeber, *Debt*, 18.

5   Graeber, *Debt*, 19.

6   Graeber, *Debt*, 18.

7   Graeber, *Debt*, 130.

8   Graeber, *Debt*, 381.

9   Graeber, *Debt*, 383.

SECTION 1
INFLUENCES

THE AUTHOR AND THE HISTORICAL CONTEXT

KEY POINTS

- David Graeber's *Debt: The First 5,000 Years* challenges our assumptions about modern economic life at a time when the world is rocked with economic crises.

- Graeber was born in New York 1961 to a family of working-class intellectuals who participated in revolutionary* and anarchist* movements: a revolutionary movement is dedicated to the overthrow of an existing political system of governance or authority; anarchism is the political philosophy that government should be abolished altogether.

- Graeber's education in anthropology*—the systematic study of humanity, especially culture and society—was heavily influenced by his conviction, inspired by the global debt and energy crises in the 1970s and 1980s, that the world is characterized by harsh and unequal power dynamics.

Why Read This Text?

David Graeber's *Debt: The First 5,000 Years* investigates the history and morality of debt with enormous breadth and detail. Published in 2011, the book was written in the immediate aftermath of the 2008 global financial crisis,* an event caused by the collapse of the American housing bubble which resulted in mass defaults on debts, affecting financial institutions and markets worldwide, and in the midst of the European debt crisis* (in which several member states have been unable to repay loans to private and public creditors).

> **❝ My childhood was full of radical politics. ❞**
> David Graeber, Interview in *Radical History Review*

These two crises together have exposed the weakest points of a consumer economy based on credit* (borrowing) and debt, national economies built on financing debt of other nations, and a global economy based on balancing the effects of imports and exports between countries. The common thread through all of these layers of economic woe is debt—which makes Graeber's work extremely relevant for students of the social sciences and members of the public alike.

The author is the first to write a popular book that considers economic questions from an anthropological perspective. By introducing this approach in a book written for a non-academic audience, Graeber has popularized the idea of taking interdisciplinary* approaches (approaches that draw on the aims and methods of different academic fields) to economic issues. On a more fundamental level, however, Graeber's book seeks to challenge the popular understanding of economics,* and to undermine the central principles of the social and economic system of capitalism* itself (a system in which trade and production are held in private hands and exercised for private profit). Graeber's views have been taken up by anti-capitalist intellectuals and activists alike, and provide sophisticated and understandable arguments for rethinking the capitalist system.

Author's Life

David Graeber was born in New York in 1961. The son of working-class intellectuals active in labor union* circles (organizations of workers founded to guarantee things such as fair pay and decent working conditions), he was exposed to leftist politics* at an early age. Graeber's mother was a garment worker. His father was affiliated with the Young Communist League* as a student and later participated in the Spanish Revolution* and Spanish Civil War* of the 1930s, in which supporters of the extreme right-wing regime of the military leader Francisco Franco* fought a coalition of Spanish and international volunteers who wanted to preserve the previous, democratic, regime.

Graeber began to declare himself an anarchist at the age of 16.[1] He graduated from the State University of New York at Purchase in 1984, then studied anthropology as a graduate student at the University of Chicago. While there he won a prestigious Fulbright Fellowship* to conduct ethnographic* research into the culture of the people of Madagascar, an island nation east of Africa. Graeber received his doctorate in anthropology in 1997.

Graeber's involvement in political activism began in 1999, when he joined protests against the World Trade Organization (WTO)* meeting in Seattle. The WTO promotes and regulates global trade, and is a symbol of the growing connections among nations around the world. Graeber established himself as a vocal figure in the global justice movement,* an international network of activist groups opposed to capitalism and globalization.* In 2011, he became an intellectual leader within Occupy Wall Street (OWS),* an activist group that grew out of a local protest in a park in New York City. Among other things, OWS protested against debt-relief policies that they believe unfairly favored wealthy creditors.* Graeber is sometimes credited for coming up with the group's now famous protest slogan "We are the 99%."[2] Today, Graeber is a professor of anthropology at the London School of Economics* and continues to participate in social activism.

Author's Background

David Graeber was a teenager in the 1970s, a period bookended by major disruptions in the global economic order. In 1971, the United States began a process that led to the end of the gold standard,* under which the US dollar and other currencies had been linked to a fixed amount of gold. In 1979, an energy crisis* caused by interruptions in the supply of petroleum from the Middle East and faltering economies in the West saw fuel prices rise sharply, creating economic hardship throughout the economy.

While Graeber was a university student, the world saw a debt crisis in the 1980s* triggered by unregulated lending from global banks to governments in developing countries* that borrowed (and sometimes wasted) more money than they could repay. In response, global trade and development organizations—the International Monetary Fund (IMF)* and the World Bank*—forced changes that created hardships for citizens of developing countries reliant on suddenly unaffordable public welfare programs and local jobs. In exchange for high-interest loans that saved them from default, these developing countries had to focus more of their budgets on loan repayment, and open their economies to international trade. According to the anthropologist Keith Hart,* "Graeber's internationalism was shaped by this wholesale looting" of developing countries.[3]

Graeber's doctoral fieldwork in Madagascar also played a considerable role in informing his politics. His views on economic inequality arose from his research on the slave trade, colonialism,* and postcolonial power struggles between Madagascar and wealthier nations. All of these aspects of Graeber's background fuel his political activism and inform the tone of *Debt* and his other academic work.

NOTES

1   Stuart Jeffries, "David Graeber Interview: 'So Many People Spend Their Working Lives Doing Jobs They Think Are Unnecessary,'" *Guardian*, March 21, 2015, http://www.theguardian.com/books/2015/mar/21/books-interview-david-graeber-the-utopia-of-rules.

2   David Runciman, "*The Democracy Project: A History, a Crisis, a Movement* by David Graeber – Review," *Guardian*, March 28, 2013, http://www.theguardian.com/books/2013/mar/28/democracy-project-david-graeber-review.

3   Keith Hart, "In Rousseau's footsteps: David Graeber and the Anthropology of Unequal Society," *The Memory Bank*, July 4, 2012, http://thememorybank.co.uk/2012/07/04/in-rousseaus-footsteps-david-graeber-and-the-anthropology-of-unequal-society-2/.

ACADEMIC CONTEXT

KEY POINTS

- The discipline of economic history* is concerned with understanding how and why economies develop.

- The common understanding within economics* and economic history has always been that debt and money arose to make buying and selling easier than in a barter* system, where trades are made directly and each party has to have something the other wants.

- David Graeber is an anthropologist*—a scholar of human culture and society—who seeks to disprove this understanding of money and debt, and to argue that non-market* societies (societies in which trade for private profit is not a defining feature) are not only possible, but perhaps better.

The Work in its Context

While David Graeber, author of *Debt: The First 5,000 Years*, is an anthropologist, his book falls mainly within the field of economic history. The book is an attempt to rethink the way that economic history has approached the subject of debt, and in doing so it draws conclusions about economic systems that depend on repayment of debts.

Whereas economics can be defined as the study of how people behave when faced with scarce means and unlimited desires, economic history is the study of this behavior, its systems, and related institutions over time. Economic history explains how and why economies have developed, and so its core concern is what economic systems and institutions have shown to be both possible and sustainable.

Debt covers a wide range of subjects, but frames all of them within

> **❝** When economists speak of the origins of money, for example, debt is always something of an afterthought ... For almost a century, anthropologists like me have been pointing out that there is something very wrong with this picture. The standard economic-history version has little to do with anything we observe when we examine how economic life is actually conducted. **❞**
>
> David Graeber, *Debt: The First 5,000 Years*

the history of debt.[1] We measure debt in monetary terms, so "A history of debt," Graeber writes, "is thus necessarily a history of money."[2] Studying the history of money helps us understand its true function, and gives us a way to consider its legitimacy as a basis for economic relations. This is an important element of *Debt*.

Overview of the Field

Economic history is a young discipline, recognized as such only in the twentieth century.[3] But the history of money has been studied as far back as ancient Greece; the philosopher Aristotle* concluded around 350 b.c.e. that money arose as means to improve the barter system:[4] a "placeholder" for goods making barter more convenient for parties without mutually desired goods. The eighteenth-century Scottish thinker Adam Smith* supported this theory in his book The Wealth of Nations (1776), the first work of modern economics.[5] In the early twentieth century it was taken up by economists of the Austrian School* (a school of economic thought that focuses on the rationality and actions of individuals as the primary forces in an economy), notably the Austrian economist Carl Menger.*[6] This theory of money remains dominant to this day, and supports the idea that money is simply an extension of humanity's natural tendency, as Adam Smith called it, to "truck and barter."

Another theory of the history of money was first put forward in the early twentieth century by the German economist Georg Friedrich Knapp,* and came to be known as chartalism.*[7] Knapp proposed that money is a "creature of law,"[8] a form of credit* that originated with states' attempts to direct market activity. Chartalism is closely related to the credit theory of money,* pioneered by the British economist Alfred Mitchell-Innes,*[9] which considers money a form of credit and debt. Chartalism and the credit theory of money were highly influential[10] in developing today's dominant understanding of an economic system, known as Keynesianism,* based on the idea that total spending is the most powerful force in the economy. But the common understanding of the origin of money continues to be that it emerged as an improvement on the barter system.

Regardless of the origin of money, most mainstream economists believe money reflects a natural human tendency for people to trade with each other.

Academic Influences

By disputing what he called the "Myth of Barter,"* David Graeber draws on the work of anthropologists before him. Marcel Mauss,* a nineteenth-century French sociologist considered to be a pioneer in anthropology, proposed in his book *The Gift* that barter was not a natural or necessary method of exchange in human society.[11] In "Barter and Economic Disintegration," the renowned British anthropologist Caroline Humphrey* wrote: "No example of a barter economy, pure and simple, has ever been described, let alone the emergence from it of money; all available [studies of the world's peoples] suggests that there never has been such a thing."[12]

The British anthropologist Keith Hart* has also contributed much to the field's scholarship on money. In his 1986 essay "Heads or Tails? Two Sides of the Coin," Hart argues that money has always been both a commodity* (something that can be traded), and a token of debt. Graeber has stated that Hart's essay was one of the inspirations for Debt.[13]

Debt also draws on unorthodox theorists like the influential German political philosopher Karl Marx,* who in his classic book Capital (1867–94)[14] warned that capitalism uses debt to oppress people, and the Hungarian American economic historian Karl Polanyi,* who in his book *The Great Transformation* (1944) suggested that markets are artificial concepts that were entirely created by the power of the state.[15] As a result, Debt draws on a wide variety of academic traditions.

NOTES

1   David Graeber, *Debt: The First 5,000 Years* (Brooklyn, NY: Melville House, 2011), 18.

2   Graeber, *Debt*, 21.

3   T. C. Barker, "The Beginnings of the Economic History Society," *The Economic History Review* 30, no. 1 (February, 1977): 4.

4   Shahzavar Karimzadi, *Money and Its Origins* (Abingdon: Routledge, 2013), 213.

5   A. Mitchell Innes, "What Is Money?," *The Banking Journal* 30 (1913): 377–408.

6   Graeber, *Debt*, 28

7   Graeber, *Debt*, 48.

8   Georg Friedrich Knapp, *The State Theory of Money* (London: Macmillan & Company, 1924), 1.

9   A. Mitchell Innes, "The Credit Theory of Money," *The Banking Journal* 31 (1914): 151–68.

10 John Maynard Keynes, *A Treatise on Money* (New York: Harcourt, Brace, & Co, 1930), 4.

11 Marcel Mauss, *The Gift* (London: Cohen & West, 1954).

12 Caroline Humphrey, "Barter and Economic Disintegration," *Man* 20, no. 1 (March, 1985): 48.

13 Keith Hart, "Heads or Tails? Two Sides of the Coin," *Man* 21, no. 4 (December, 1986): 637–56.

14 Karl Marx, *Das Kapital* (Chicago: Charles H. Kerr & Co, 1906).

15 Karl Polanyi, *The Great Transformation* (Boston: Beacon Press, 1944).

MODULE 3
THE PROBLEM

KEY POINTS

- The main question concerning academics at the time of *Debt's* publication is whether the current capitalist* system, in which trade and production are conducted for private profit, is fair to debtors.

- Economists differ as to whether debt should be seen as the greatest threat to economic growth, whereas popular activist movements argue that capitalism itself perpetuates injustice through debt.

- David Graeber uses scholarly arguments from outside the discipline of economics* to criticize capitalism.

Core Question

In *Debt: The First 5,000 Years*, David Graeber is attempting to answer several questions, some of which are academic and some of which are moral. All of them lead to the core question: "What, in terms of economic life, is a fair way to live?" After the global financial crisis 2008,* this was a major concern for many economists and policy makers.

As Graeber recalls: "After 2008, for example, there was this moment that lasted maybe a month or so, where suddenly you could talk about anything. Everything was in doubt. Even *The Economist** ran headlines effectively asking: 'Capitalism: was it a good idea?' Obviously, they concluded yes; they're *The Economist*. But, nonetheless, it seemed like everything was up for grabs. You could think big thoughts again and wonder why it was all here. Why do we have an economy? And that lasted about four weeks, until everyone said, 'Shut up and stop thinking

> ❝ This book is a history of debt, then, but it also uses that history as a way to ask fundamental questions about what human beings and human society are or could be like—what do we actually owe each other, and what it even means to ask that question. ❞
>
> David Graeber, *Debt: The First 5,000 Years*

about this. It will come back if we just close our eyes and ears and keep carrying on as if nothing is happening."[1]

Ultimately, Graeber gives only an indirect answer to the core question, by arguing that our ideas of debt and fairness under capitalism are problematic. In doing so, he opens the door for new ways of considering the issue in the future.

The Participants

Another question related to Graeber's focus—the question of how to reconcile our ideas of debt under capitalism with harsh realities for debtors—was part of a raging debate at the time of *Debt*'s publication. One camp, consisting primarily of Western politicians and economic institutions founded to provide loans and financial assistance for developing countries* (the International Monetary Fund* and the World Bank*), and backed by the American economists Carmen Reinhart* and Kenneth Rogoff,*[2] maintained that high levels of debt were bad for economic growth. They also argued that rescuing debtors by forgiving debt would encourage more irresponsible behavior (a principle described as "moral hazard"), so the debts should be paid back. The opposing camp, consisting of most mainstream economists in the academic world and including prominent Keynesians* like the Nobel Prize-winning economists Paul Krugman* and Amartya Sen,* supported some concessions for debt relief. They also argued that forcing developing countries to reduce government spending until debts are repaid would be a bigger barrier to economic growth. According to Keynesian thought, a country's economic output, in the short run, is influenced by the economy's level of total demand.

At the same time, activist movements driven by anger over economic inequality were rallying on the fringes of the academic and policy debates. These movements, including the global justice movement* (a network of international social activist movements that oppose corporate globalization*) and, later, the Occupy movement (a global protest movement against economic and social inequality that began in 2011), were joined by radical economists like the French scholar Thomas Piketty* in extending the pro-debt relief position to its most extreme. They argued that capitalism itself was unjust, as it reinforced inequality and took away the rights of debtors.[3] Graeber's work reflects this belief.

The Contemporary Debate

The debate continues between those who want to change the treatment of debt within the framework of capitalism, and those who want to rethink capitalism altogether. In Europe, there has been an extended struggle between nations over austerity* budgets (budgets that force debtor countries to reduce government spending in favor of repaying more debt). Conflict including riots in Greece over plans to reduce spending and raise taxes have led to a belief among many politicians and economists that austerity is politically unsustainable as a solution to financial turmoil.[4]

At the same time, the activist movements have lost momentum because of an inability to organize themselves around a clear platform. Debt is considered important because the book pulls together the academic ideas behind the activism. Another such book is Thomas Piketty's *Capital in the Twenty-First Century*—although *Debt* goes further than *Capital* in urging that capitalism as a system be reconsidered. Graeber's anarchist* politics* (his position that governments should be abolished) and association with Occupy Wall Street* and the global justice movement draw him into the contemporary debate and position him as an anti-capitalist intellectual.

NOTES

1   Hannah Chadeayne Appel, "Finance Is Just Another Word for Other People's Debts: An Interview with David Graeber," *Radical History Review*, no. 118 (2014): 168.

2   Carmen M. Reinhart and Kenneth S. Rogoff, "Growth in a Time of Debt," *American Economic Review* 100, no. 2 (May, 2010): 573–8.

3   Thomas Piketty, *Capital in the Twenty-First Century* (Cambridge, MA: Harvard University Press, 2014).

4   Amartya Sen, "The Economic Consequences of Austerity," *New Statesman*, June 4, 2015.

MODULE 4
THE AUTHOR'S CONTRIBUTION

KEY POINTS

- Graeber believes we can build an idea of a fairer economic life using anthropological* evidence (evidence drawn from the study of human culture and society) comparing market* societies (defined by the extent to which trade is conducted for private profit) and non-market societies.

- Graeber's exploration of debt introduces anthropology into a public debate that has largely occurred within the confines of economics* and economic history.*

- *Debt* summarizes and builds on a century-old body of work known as economic anthropology* (the study of the ways in which different human cultures conduct their economic affairs).

Author's Aims

David Graeber has several aims in *Debt: The First 5,000 Years*. At a basic level, he wants to clear up the "profound moral confusion"[1] about what debt actually is by building a definition of debt that is free from "the logic of the marketplace."[2]

He wants to advance the discipline of anthropology by injecting its insights into a discussion usually associated with economic theory and economic history. As such, the book practices a kind of intellectual sabotage that systematically undermines the work of the eighteenth-century economist Adam Smith* and his descendants, and strengthens the position of Graeber's own intellectual forebears in the field of economic anthropology along the way.

At the broadest level, however, Graeber is trying to promote anti-capitalism* by means of relevant and serious scholarship without falling back on the outmoded ideas of Karl Marx* or the fringes of

> ❝ One of the puzzling things about all the theories on the origins of money that we've been looking at so far is that they almost completely ignore the evidence of anthropology. ❞
>
> David Graeber, *Debt: The First 5,000 Years*

leftist extremism. Graeber does not make any sweeping policy proposals, other than offering the idea of extensive debt relief.[3] But he clearly intends to inspire others to create solutions once they have set aside their commitment to capitalism.

Approach

In *Debt*, Graeber does not build arguments on top of preexisting economic theory or political philosophy. He seeks only to disprove existing arguments. Graeber believes capitalism evolved because of a series of events in world history, and is not based on any objective economic truths. Based on this approach, he reveals lessons about debt, morality, and markets by examining economic history in detail.

Graeber bases his work on evidence, and is thorough in referencing his sources. But the sheer size of the time period covered (3500 b.c.e. to the present) forces him to trot briskly through historical and anthropological evidence, providing his own opinions and theories where they are relevant. As a result, the book's chapters are not neatly tied to a central point. Graeber quickly lays out some of his arguments at the beginning and provides the evidence to support them as he goes along, making other key arguments at the end.

While this would be a problem in an academic paper, the approach works well in a book written for a popular audience. Graeber values storytelling over technicalities, so that the reader finishes with a clear set of ideas and opinions and plenty of examples to support them. But it is difficult to stitch all the ideas together into a consistent theory.

Contribution in Context

One of Debt's unique contributions is that it combines the various traditions in economic anthropology in an effort to disprove the traditional understanding of economics. Graeber pulls together an enormous range of ethnographic* (cultural) studies, physical evidence from earlier societies, and anthropological theory to conclude that money did not originate from barter* (trade without money) and did not arise as a unit of exchange.

He also supports the school of thought pioneered by the British anthropologist Keith Hart,* who said money has always been both a commodity* (something valuable in its own right) and a tool for credit,* and debt accounting. Graeber builds on Hart's views by arguing that over history, civilization has swung back and forth between credit and commodity forms of money. When Graeber told Hart of this claim in person, Hart acknowledged that he had never realized that before.

Graeber also discusses why money really came about, if not for exchange. He then draws moral conclusions from this discussion, arguing that economies have manipulated the concepts of credit and debt by using money to enforce power relationships. While Graeber does not describe a new anti-capitalist anthropological theory, he assembles many of the pieces needed to do so.

NOTES

1   David Graeber, *Debt: The First 5,000 Years* (Brooklyn, NY: Melville House, 2011), 8.

2   Graeber, *Debt*, 90.

3   Graeber, *Debt*, 390.

SECTION 2
IDEAS

MAIN IDEAS

KEY POINTS

- David Graeber writes about two key themes in *Debt:* the origin of money and markets,* and the origins of the concept of "debt" itself.

- According to Graeber, money and markets are tools artificially created to convert the social obligations on which human relationships are built into measureable "debts" people in a position of power can use to take advantage of others.

- *Debt* is written for a popular audience, so while making its arguments it provides easily understandable discussions on morality and political philosophy.

Key Themes

David Graeber wants to understand whether our current economic system, centered on the idea of debt, is truly fair; the title *Debt: The First 5,000 Years* makes it plain that debt will be the central focus of the work. His attempts to answer the question "What is debt?" are a tool for the teaching of many lessons about the economy.

Debt addresses three themes that work together to build a clear idea of what debt really is:

- The "myth" that exchange is the most important feature of human behavior
- The role of "obligation" in creating moral grounds for economic relations
- The artificiality of financial debt in human history.

Each of these three themes reveals something important about debt. Graeber says that, within the language of exchange, debt is a transaction

> ❝ Not only is it money that makes debt possible: money and debt appear on the scene at exactly the same time. ❞
>
> David Graeber, *Debt: The First 5,000 Years*

that has not yet been completed. He also says, however, that this is not the natural way for human beings to frame their interactions with one another. Finally, Graeber cites historical evidence in arguing that financial debt in particular is an artificial idea that distorts the nature of social obligations to turn them into part of the market economy.

Exploring the Ideas

One of the core principles of economics* is that human beings relate to one another on the basis of exchange. In *Debt*, Graeber seeks to disprove this by discrediting three supporting "myths."

The first, referred to as "the Myth of Barter,"* is the eighteenth-century economist Adam Smith's* notion that money arose to facilitate barter.* "The Myth of Barter cannot go away because it is central to the discourse of economics," Graeber writes.[1] But there is, however, no evidence in the historical record nor in anthropological* fieldwork to suggest that barter predates the creation of money, or that it played an important role in creating money.[2]

The second myth is that of "primordial debts,"* meaning debts that have always existed. According to primordial debt theory: "Governments use taxes to create money, and they are able to do so because they have become the guardians of the debt that all citizens have to one another. This debt is the essence of society itself … and money and markets themselves are simply ways of chopping pieces of it up."[3] Like barter, primordial debt suggests that people interpret their relationships as transactions. Graeber rejects primordial debt as a myth that claims money itself is a tribute to state power. He cites anthropological evidence showing that money not only existed in non-market societies for ritualistic purposes, but that even in market societies the function of money was dictated by both the state and the market.

The latter point speaks to the third myth—that the market and the state are independent from each other. Graeber argues that, in fact, the two "were born together and have always been intertwined."[4] Money as a unit of account originated in the temple and palace complexes of the world's earliest urban civilization, Mesopotamia,* more than 3,000 years b.c.e. During the Axial Age* (a period of ancient history characterized by great advances in human philosophical thought, normally considered to have lasted from 800 b.c.e. to 200 b.c.e.), aggressive states throughout Eurasia* looking to expand began issuing money in the form of coins to soldiers. The rulers of these states then demanded that citizens pay taxes using the same coins, which forced citizens to sell supplies to soldiers in exchange for the coins to pay taxes. Markets emerged as a result.

As Graeber puts it, the above three myths all "tend to reduce all human relations to exchange, as if our ties to society … can be imagined in the same terms as a business deal."[5] Graeber tries to upend these myths and suggests that exchange is not the most natural sense of indebtedness in human relationships.

Graeber's second theme describes the differences between exchange-related debt and other obligations. Graeber argues that people organize their sense of obligation in three ways, based on:

- Communism* (looking out for one another according to abilities and needs)
- Exchange (impersonally trading things of similar value)
- Hierarchy (interaction between an inferior and superior).

People shift between these approaches based on the nature of their relationships,[6] and exchange tends to be reserved for strangers.

Finally, Graeber argues that debt is artificial by tracing how the nature of money has changed throughout history. He presents a vast discussion of the history of Eurasia split into four stages:

- The Age of the First Agrarian Empires (3500–800 B.C.E.; "agrarian empires" were political bodies with economies founded on agriculture)
- The Axial Age (800 B.C.E.–600 C.E.)
- The Middle Ages (600–1450 C.E.)
- The "Age of the Great Capitalist Empires" (1450 C.E. to the present day).

Depending on the politics* of the era,[7] money alternates in form during these stages between virtual (a symbol of credit*) and commodity* (a physical object that has value, usually gold). This demonstrates that debt itself is a political invention that can be redefined.

Language and Expression

Graeber has described *Debt: The First 5,000 Years* as "the sort of book people don't write any more: a big book, asking big questions, meant to be read widely and spark public debate, but at the same time, without any sacrifice of scholarly rigor."[8] This is reflected in the fact that 149 of the book's 542 pages consist of endnotes and references, a feature more common in textbooks than in books for a mass audience.

At the same time, Graeber intended for *Debt* to be "an accessible work, written in plain English, that actually does try to challenge common sense assumptions."[9] In a disorganized but ultimately pleasant way, the book eases the popular audience into centuries-long intellectual debates in economics and philosophy, and provides a vast wealth of data collected from anthropological fieldwork. As an activist himself, Graeber believes the broader public should take part in discussions on debt and its moral implications, rather than just scholars and policy makers.

NOTES

1   David Graeber, *Debt: The First 5,000 Years* (Brooklyn, NY: Melville House, 2001), 43.

2   Graeber, *Debt*, 28.

3   Graeber, *Debt*, 56.

4   Graeber, *Debt*, 18.

5   Graeber, *Debt*, 18.

6   Graeber, *Debt*, 113.

7   Graeber, *Debt*, 213.

8   David Graeber, "Can We Still Write Big Question Sorts of Books?" *Savage Minds*, July 31, 2011, http://savageminds.org/2011/07/31/can-we-still-write-big-question-sorts-of-books/.

9   Graeber, "Big Question Sorts of Books."

MODULE 6
SECONDARY IDEAS

KEY POINTS

- Graeber argues that money has always been a fluid concept, used as both a symbol or representation of credit* and as a tradable commodity* (a physical object, such as gold).

- He adds a moral dimension to his arguments by saying there is a pattern of violence associated with debt, and that the capitalist* system is designed to help the wealthy and powerful take advantage of others.

- Graeber connects the rise and fall of currency and the rise and fall of slavery throughout human history as an extreme example of the dangers of money and debt.

Other Ideas

An important secondary idea in David Graeber's *Debt: The First 5,000 Years* is the relationship between debt, markets, * and violence. Graeber explores this through his concept of the "human economy."

One of the main ideas of *Debt* is that our current economic system is not legitimate because it is built on the idea that debt is simply an impersonal exchange that is not yet complete. Graeber argues that exchange-related debt is part of a broader system of more personal obligations. By artificially reducing debt to an amount of money and insisting on repayment, the economic system alienates people from each other.

In *Debt*, Graeber also argues that the modern economic system centered on debt is actually harmful. This means the book is not just an alternative to mainstream economic history,* but also thoroughly anti-

> **" The crucial factor ... is money's capacity to turn morality into a matter of impersonal arithmetic—and by doing so, to justify things that would otherwise seem outrageous or obscene. "**
> David Graeber, *Debt: The First 5,000 Years*

capitalist. This is in line with Graeber's own politics,* and provides academic justification for his participation in activist movements.

Exploring the Ideas

In Chapter Six of *Debt*, Graeber introduces the concept of "human economies," which differs from the more familiar commercial or market economy. Human economies, according to Graeber, mainly exist before or outside of market systems and are "primarily concerned not with the accumulation of wealth, but with the creation, destruction, and rearranging of human beings."[1] In these economies, "each person is unique, and of incomparable value, because each is a unique nexus of relations with others."[2] Anthropological* evidence shows that in the human economy money exists, but that it is not used in routine transactions for goods and services. Rather, it is used in a ritual way in situations dealing with matters of great importance that cannot be calculated. In these pre-market economies, money is a way to "arrange marriages, establish the paternity of children, head off feuds, console mourners at funerals, seek forgiveness in the case of crimes, negotiate treaties—almost anything but trade…"[3]

This all changes, however, when people are removed from their familiar realities, usually through violence. As Graeber writes, even in the human economy "humans can become objects of exchange: first, perhaps, women given in marriage; ultimately, slaves captured in war. What all these relations have in common [is] violence."[4] Anthropology and history reveal, according to Graeber, that "It is only by the threat of sticks, ropes, spears, and guns that one can tear people out of those endlessly complicated webs of relationships with others … that render them unique, and thus reduce them to something that can be traded."[5] This is how physical forms of money change from ritual objects into tools for the commodification and exchange of human beings.

In the human economy, routine interactions with trusted people take the form of communism* or hierarchy. Exchange comes about through violence, or the threat of violence. This can take the mild form of distrust or fear between two people exchanging objects, or the much harsher form of the exchange of people through slavery.

When human economies are taken over or changed into commercial economies, violence increases. Graeber gives examples of this point throughout his book:

- The violent commodification of people as slaves in pre-market societies
- The introduction of coins to fuel war machines in the Axial Age*
- Today, the forced repossession of homes to make good on bank debts.

Debt asks the question "What is debt?" Graeber answers in the last paragraph of his book: "A debt is just the perversion of a promise. It is a promise corrupted by both math and violence."[6]

Overlooked

Graeber's discussion of the primordial debt* theory is both his least developed and most overlooked. As the cultural anthropologist Bill Maurer has written, "Everyone is captivated by [Graeber's] critique of the myth of primitive barter.* Yet it is a puzzle that a core element of his argument—the myth of primordial debt—has been largely overlooked."[7]

The "Myth of Barter"* is the idea that money arose spontaneously as a solution to the inconveniences of barter; it is possible to approach the truth of this proposition by testing evidence. But "primordial debt" is a philosophical idea, resistant to similar analysis; the primary sources we must turn to are ancient scriptures. Referring to sacred texts of the Indian Hindu tradition written in about 800 b.c.e., Graeber writes that "two famous passages in the Brahmanas* insist that we are born as a debt not just to the gods, to be repaid in sacrifice … but also to the Sages … which we must repay through study; to our ancestors, who we must repay by having children; and finally, 'to men'—apparently meaning humanity as a whole, to be repaid by offering hospitality to strangers."[8] Primordial debt theorists say these ideas "are not peculiar to a certain intellectual tradition [but are] essential to the very nature and history of human thought."[9]

As Graeber says, by thinking about how to repay an "infinite debt" we are saddled with at birth, "the Brahmanas are offering a quite sophisticated reflection on a moral question that no one has really ever been able to answer any better before or since."[10] While Graeber says he rejects the primordial debt myth, his own alternative philosophy can be read as supporting it: "If one were looking for the ethos for an individualistic society such as our own, one way to do it might well be to say: we all owe an infinite debt to humanity, society, nature, or the cosmos … but no one could possibly tell us how we are to pay it … Human freedom would then be our ability to decide for ourselves how we want to do so."[11]

NOTES

1   David Graeber, *Debt: The First 5,000 Years* (Brooklyn, NY: Melville House, 2001), 130.

2   Graeber, *Debt*, 158.

3   Graeber, *Debt*, 130.

4   Graeber, *Debt*, 208.

5   Graeber, *Debt*, 208.

6   Graeber, *Debt*, 391.

7   Bill Maurer, "David Graeber's Wunderkammer, *Debt: The First 5,000 Years*," *Anthropological Forum* 23, no. 1 (2013): 79.

8   Graeber, *Debt*, 57.

9   Graeber, *Debt*, 57.

10 Graeber, *Debt*, 67.

11 Graeber, *Debt*, 68.

MODULE 7
ACHIEVEMENT

KEY POINTS

- David Graeber has written a critical analysis of economics*
  and the capitalist* system that has been met with public
  praise, and brings anthropological* theories on the
  economy into the public consciousness.

- Graeber frames the book as "a big book of ideas," rather
  than a textbook, and uses anthropological evidence from
  around the world to make *Debt* broadly significant.

- The somewhat disorganized structure of the book limits
  the ability of audiences to follow Graeber's arguments,
  and the fact that Graeber has no background in economics
  limits the willingness of economists to take the book
  seriously.

Assessing the Argument

David Graeber's *Debt: The First 5,000 Years* tries to combine the
resources of a wide range of academic disciplines to change the way
people think about economics. But the task requires a level of
organizational skill that the work does not, it might be argued,
perfectly achieve. Graeber reasons through two types of discussion:

- Using direct evidence from human history to challenge the
  common understanding of economics
- Discussing moral issues in a Socratic* manner (that is, through
  posing and answering questions in a manner associated with the
  ancient Greek philosopher Socrates).

He weaves between these modes somewhat indiscriminately, often
bringing a moral discussion related to one topic into a description of
history related to a different topic. Graeber also begins most of his

> **" David has become something of a cult figure in anthropology now. "**
>
> James Scott, professor of political science and anthropology,
> Yale University

chapters by stating the topic clearly at the beginning, and then abandoning it. For example, he starts Chapter Eight by saying that throughout Eurasian* history, money switched back and forth between periods when it was taken as credit*—a symbol—and periods when it was a commodity*—gold, for example.[1] But it is hard to follow this through the sweeping historical discussion that ensues; meanwhile, he confuses matters by making moral points about violence and repression.

The disorganization of the book makes it hard to grasp Graeber's central point—that under capitalism,* debt is a perversion of social obligations used to justify violence. The necessary arguments and information are there, but readers are required to stitch it together themselves.

Achievement in Context

The structural weaknesses of *Debt* have not kept it from becoming a prominent work of nonfiction. The "big book of ideas" produced by an established academic for a broad audience was (and remains) popular. As a genre, *Debt* follows in the footsteps of *Guns, Germs, and Steel*, an equally vast work by the scientist and author Jared Diamond.* *Guns, Germs, and Steel* pushed geography* as an academic discipline into the debates of economic historians* in much the same way that Graeber intends for anthropology. Nearly 20 years after its publication in 1997, Diamond's book continues to have considerable influence as a contribution to the theory of "path dependency"*—the idea that states develop along a certain path because of predetermined factors like geography.

Debt was an international bestseller in the year after its publication (2011).[2] So far, no one has challenged the factuality of the historical and anthropological evidence Graber presents, even while debating the conclusions he draws from that evidence. This suggests that *Debt* could become a respected academic work just as it has captured the public imagination, although more gradually and after long processes of peer review.

Limitations

Graeber intends to incorporate global history and anthropology into Debt and apply them to the universal human experience. To the extent that he is successful, his reflections on economic life are not limited by geography or the present historical period. Graeber's background as an anthropologist helps him reach out to a broad audience, because he is in the business of understanding the similarities and differences between people from different backgrounds. Debt's individual claims are meant to remain sound and logical even as they thread their way through different cultures.

At the same time, the work's greatest limitation is in its title—a declaration that it is only looking backward. While the book combines various insights into a value judgment on capitalism as a whole, that is not enough to lead to any policy prescriptions, beyond the single suggestion of providing more debt relief. It might be argued that this hinders Debt from making a wholly constructive contribution to the debate.

NOTES

1   David Graeber, *Debt: The First 5,000 Years* (Brooklyn, NY: Melville House, 2011), 212.

2   Keith Hart, "In Rousseau's Footsteps: David Graeber and the Anthropology of Unequal Society," *The Memory Bank*, July 4, 2012, http://thememorybank.co.uk/2012/07/04/in-rousseaus-footsteps-david-graeber-and-the-anthropology-of-unequal-society-2/.

PLACE IN THE AUTHOR'S WORK

KEY POINTS

- Graeber's overall scholarship focuses on the more radical topics of economic anthropology,* including equality, power dynamics, and revolution.*

- *Debt* is an extension of Graeber's previous work on anthropological theories of value,* in which he questions the ability of the capitalist* system to accurately value the contributions of human beings to one another.

- The anti-capitalist nature of Debt supports Graeber's reputation as a rebel and lends intellectual strength to his political leanings as an anarchist.*

Positioning

Debt: The First 5,000 Years builds heavily on David Graeber's previous scholarship and the development of his political ideas throughout his scholarly career. It also represents a change in Graeber's scholarly direction, in which he turns away from the pure anthropology and ethnography* (field study of a people's culture or society) that characterized his work in most of the 2000s to revisit the economic anthropology of his first book, *Toward an Anthropological Theory of Value* (2001).

In many ways *Debt* is a logical extension of *Toward an Anthropological Theory of Value*. *Debt* uses one of *Toward's* core arguments—the inability of the capitalist market* to accurately value human actions—as an intellectual backdrop. To underwrite his analysis of debt, Graeber musters a great deal of evidence from his previous works in anthropology and his own research.

> **❝** Anthropology seems a discipline terrified of its own potential. **❞**
>
> David Graeber, *Fragments of an Anarchist Anthropology*

Integration

One of *Debt's* major themes is the argument that the capitalist system uses debt as a mechanism to perpetuate inequality and abuse. This is rooted in Graeber's doctoral fieldwork on the island of Madagascar, where he witnessed first hand the negative effects of large amounts of government debt on economy and people. Pressure to repay the national debt served as both moral and practical justification for cutting social welfare programs and harming quality of life. Later, in 2007, Graeber would also publish *Lost People: Magic and the Legacy of Slavery in Madagascar*. Although a purely anthropological work with a narrow focus on Madagascar, it nonetheless introduced many of the ideas on slavery, inequality, and debt that serve as secondary themes in *Debt*.[1]

The most direct influence on *Debt* from within Graeber's own body of work, however, comes from *Toward an Anthropological Theory of Value*, Graeber's first book, which established him as an anthropologist concerned with the issues of economic theory. The book's basic position is that people and, by extension, their actions are the most important "products" of a society.[2] The implication is that the notion that values can be established through market exchange is simply wrong: the basis for Graeber's exploration of debt and human economies in Debt.

Significance

Graeber was already considered one of the greatest anthropologists of his generation well before the publication of *Debt*. His extensive ethnographic work on Madagascar, which ranged from his time as a graduate student to his publication of Lost People, was highly regarded within his field.[3] After the publication of Graeber's books *Toward an Anthropological Theory of Value and Fragments of an Anarchist Anthropology*, the British anthropologist Maurice Bloch* wrote: "[Graeber's] writings on anthropological theory are outstanding. I consider him the best anthropological theorist of his generation from anywhere in the world."[4]

Graeber's significant body of anthropological writing on power relations, hierarchies, and activism, bookended by *Toward an Anthropological Theory of Value* and *Debt*: the First 5,000 Years, positions Graeber as a pioneering intellectual in what the anthropologist Keith Hart* calls "anthropology of unequal society."[5] Of all his work, *Debt* has received the most critical acclaim, winning the Bateson Book Prize from the Society for Cultural Anthropology and the Bread and Roses Award from the Alliance of Radical Booksellers.

NOTES

1   David Graeber, *Debt: The First 5,000 Years* (Brooklyn, NY: Melville House, 2011), 4.

2   David Graeber, *Toward an Anthropological Theory of Value: The False Coin of Our Own Dreams* (New York: Palgrave Macmillan, 2001).

3   Thomas Meaney, "Anarchist Anthropology," *The New York Times*, December 8, 2011, http://www.nytimes.com/2011/12/11/books/review/anarchist-anthropology.html.

4   Maurice Bloch, "Letter from Maurice Bloch, London School of Economics" (2005).

5   Keith Hart, "In Rousseau's Footsteps: David Graeber and the Anthropology of Unequal Society," *The Memory Bank*, July 4, 2012, http://thememorybank.co.uk/2012/07/04/in-rousseaus-footsteps-david graeber-and-the-anthropology-of-unequal-society-2/.

SECTION 3
IMPACT

THE FIRST RESPONSES

KEY POINTS

- The principal criticisms made of *Debt* are that David Graeber has not adequately understood the internal debates among economists, that he attaches too much importance to the origins of economic ideas as a measure of their value, and that his recommendation for debt relief is impractical.

- The fact that Graeber and his detractors come from different disciplines (anthropology* and economics,* respectively) makes it difficult for the two to engage in a substantive debate.

- Graeber's ideas have been well received by economists outside the mainstream.

Criticism

Debt: The First 5,000 Years was a controversial book at the time of its publication; while David Graeber's ideas have been ignored by most economists, a few have expressed opposition or support. Among those who chose to critically engage with *Debt*, Noah Smith* and Mike Beggs* offer the most detailed criticisms.

Smith, an assistant professor of finance at Stony Brook University and a popular economics writer, says that many monetary economists already recognize that credit* preceded barter.* He suggests that Graeber accuses economists of misleading the public without understanding the diversity of views within economics. Smith also argues that Graeber's proposal for debt cancellation in response to overwhelming debt levels would make lenders very unwilling to lend

> 66 5,000 years of anecdotes is no substitute for real
> political economy. 99
>
> Mike Beggs, *Jacobin*

in the future, and would reward those bold enough to take out large loans rather than those in need.[1]

Beggs, a political economy* lecturer at the University of Sydney, says Debt is a "valuable contribution,"[2] but rejects Graeber's use of history as a tool for undermining economic theory. "Economics studies a system, and origins of its parts might mislead about their present functions and dynamics," he writes. "The answer to bad economics is good economics, not no economics."[3] In opposition to Beggs, the economist J. W. Mason* has claimed that the 'big ideas' related to economics that are presented in Debt are legitimate. "Debt backs up each of them with an enormous wealth of historical material, though sometimes less than clear theoretical statements," Mason writes.[4]

Responses

Graeber has been accused by many of his detractors of being unwilling to accept any criticism. Because they are not anthropologists,* Graeber's critics have been unable to dispute the anthropological evidence he cites to dismiss the Myth of Barter;* because he is not an economist, Graeber lacks the technical knowledge to engage with the claims of economists such as Mike Beggs who accuse him of overlooking constructive solutions to debt crises from the field of economics. The result is that both Graeber and his critics are left to argue over minor points rather than the merits of the book as a whole or its broader implications.

Graeber's main response to arguments like those of Noah Smith that debt relief makes lenders unwilling to lend is that this has been disproven. As Graeber points out, history has had many instances of debt relief, and the practice of lending continues. Furthermore, "big players" (that is, the wealthy or giant corporations) forgive and restructure* one another's debts frequently.

Conflict and Consensus

Graeber and his critics argue primarily over petty scholarly points. The book was published so recently that there has not yet been time for a book or an academic work of equal academic weight to offer an opposing school of thought. The debate is largely confined to the Internet.

In the left–wing quarterly Jacobin magazine, Mike Beggs wrote that Debt is "another move in an interdisciplinary* struggle: anthropology against economics."[5] This is an accurate description, as a gulf has existed between the conclusions of anthropology and economics for approximately a century. However, there is a clear space for cooperation between Graeber's camp and economists outside the mainstream. As J. W. Mason has written: "Admittedly it takes some unpacking, but Debt's key themes are in close harmony with the main themes of heterodox economics* work going back to Keynes."[6] It is likely that future economic scholarship will incorporate the anthropological perspective.

NOTES

1   Noah Smith, "David Graeber: Debt Is Bad, or Something?," *Noahpinion*, February 13, 2013, http://noahpinionblog.blogspot.co.uk/2013/02/david-graeber-debt-is-bad-or-something.html.

2   Mike Beggs, "On Debt: A Reply to Josh Mason," *Jacobin*, September 20, 2012, https://www.jacobinmag.com/2012/09/on-debt-a-reply-to-josh-mason/.

3   Mike Beggs, "Debt: The First 500 Pages," *Jacobin*, August, 2012, 7–8.

4   J. W. Mason, "In Defense of David Graeber's Debt," *Jacobin*, September 18, 2012, https://www.jacobinmag.com/2012/09/in-defense-of-david-graebers-debt/.

5   Beggs, "Debt."

6   Mason, "In Defense of David Graeber's Debt."

MODULE 10
THE EVOLVING DEBATE

KEY POINTS

- As a book written for a popular audience, *Debt* is positioned as a key influence in shaping the layman's views on economics* and the current difficulties of the global economic system.

- Although unique in its approach, *Debt* is one of a number of books in an emerging literature and school of thought highlighting the tendency of capitalism* toward inequality.

- *Debt* presents a historical, moral, and philosophical basis for the idea of debt relief, heavily discussed today as a means of alleviating the difficulties of global financial crises.

Uses and Problems

While David Graeber's *Debt: The First 5,000 Years* has been hailed since its publication as an influential work in anthropology* and academia at large, it has found the most use in the public sphere.[1] This is in line with Graeber's intentions, as he wrote Debt thinking "it would be interesting to write for a broader audience and see what kind of impact you can have on the arguments going on."[2]

Owing to the timing of its publication in the wake of the global financial crisis,* *Debt* joins a great deal of literature written with the aim of inspiring a debate on capitalism. But while other economists and political philosophers are heavily critical of the mechanisms of the capitalist system, *Debt* launches an open attack on the ideologies driving capitalism and on the system itself. *Debt's* radicalism is currently, perhaps, what prevents the conversion of its popularity into popular action.

> **❝** If we want an alternative to stagnation, impoverishment, and ecological devastation, we're just going to have to figure out a way to unplug the machine and start again. **❞**
>
> David Graeber, *Guardian*

Schools of Thought

Scholars who have played an important role in popularizing the debate on global inequality and capitalism include the economists Thomas Piketty* of France, Joseph Stieglitz* of the United States, and Dani Rodrik* of Turkey.

By far the most successful recent book in bridging the divide between academia and the public over inequality is Thomas Piketty's *Capital in the Twenty-First Century*. This book does not call for dismantling the capitalist system, but, rather, for a serious reform of its mechanics so that global tax systems might redistribute enough wealth to undo inequality produced by capitalism.[3] Nonetheless, *Capital* shares some of *Debt's* core features, arguing against the idea that capitalism operates on principles of equality. As Knox Peden has written in the *Sydney Review of Books:* "Though Piketty and Graeber are temperamentally antipodal [opposites], the thematic resonance connecting their works is clear enough."[4]

In 2015, Piketty appeared to acknowledge Graeber's analysis when he called for an international conference on debt and the implementation of a new strategy for dealing with the European debt crisis:* "Essentially, it consists of three components: inflation,* a special tax on private wealth, and debt relief."[5]

In Current Scholarship

Brought together by a mutual frustration with inequality, Graeber and Piketty have engaged with each other directly on how to move forward the current scholarship criticizing capitalism and inequality. The two scholars approach the debate from completely different practical viewpoints.

In *Capital*, Piketty supports Graeber's idea that capitalism is a system that, in its purest form, cannot help but create injustice: "Capitalism does not contain an inherent tendency to civilize itself. Left to its own devices, it can be expected to create rates of return on investment so much higher than overall rates of economic growth that the only possible result will be to transfer more and more wealth into the hands of a hereditary elite of investors, to the comparative impoverishment of everybody else."[6]

In line with his own intellectual background and previous work, Graeber favors a revolutionary response to this problem. "Since the 1970s," he writes, "as any significant political threat has receded, things have gone back to their normal state: that is, to savage inequalities." Graeber's criticism of Piketty is that he "has nothing against capitalism itself … He just wishes to provide a check on capitalism's tendency to create a useless class of parasitical rentiers* [people who live off the profits from investments]." Graeber concludes that total debt relief and an "unplugging" of the capitalist system is in order.[7]

Piketty's response has been that Graeber's solution—to put the burden on creditors—is unjust. "The fact is, as I say, that the last creditors are not necessarily the ones who should be made to pay," Piketty has argued. Rather, a progressive tax* should be imposed on wealth, which, according to Piketty, "seems … a more civilized way to arrive at the same result."[8]

NOTES

1   Hannah Chadeayne Appel, "Finance Is Just Another Word for Other People's Debts: An Interview with David Graeber," *Radical History Review* no. 118 (2014): 168.

2   Appel, "Other People's Debts," 168.

3   Thomas Piketty and Arthur Goldhammer, *Capital in the Twenty-First Century* (Cambridge, MA: The Belknap Press of Harvard University Press, 2014).

4   Knox Peden, "The Abstractions of History," *The Sydney Review of Books*, July 22, 2014, http://www.sydneyreviewofbooks.com/capital-twenty-first-century-thomas-piketty/.

5   Gavin Schalliol, "Thomas Piketty: 'Germany Has Never Repaid Its Debts. It Has No Right to Lecture Greece,'" *The Wire*, July 8, 2015, http://thewire.in/2015/07/08/thomas-piketty-germany-has-never-repaid-its-debts-it-has-no-right-to-lecture-greece-5851/.

6   David Graeber, "Savage Capitalism Is Back—And It Will Not Tame Itself," *Guardian*, May 30, 2014, http://www.theguardian.com/commentisfree/2014/may/30/savage-capitalism-back-radical-challenge.

7   Graeber, "Savage Capitalism."

8   David Graeber and Thomas Piketty, "Soak the Rich: An Exchange on Capital, Debt, and the Future," *The Baffler*, July 31, 2014, http://thebaffler.com/odds-and-ends/soak-the-rich.

IMPACT AND INFLUENCE TODAY

KEY POINTS

- *Debt* has become a central work in the global activist community.

- The work directly challenges policymakers and other members of the international economic and governance elite to change the way that they view credit,* debt, and the morality of the capitalist* system.

- The debate between policymakers and economists is still ongoing, although those who favor debt relief believe they are gaining ground.

Position

Debt has become a "must-read" in international activist circles. Public intellectuals like Antonio Negri,* the Italian Marxist* sociologist and political philosopher, have cited Debt in their activist writings and calls for action. In their 2012 joint essay *Declaration*, Negri and American political philosopher Michael Hardt* state, "In contrast to the myth of equal exchange, then, the debtor–creditor relationship has the virtue of unmasking the vast inequalities at the foundation of capitalist society." One of their listed sources of evidence for this statement is David Graeber's *Debt: The First 5,000 Years*.

Even outside of the community of hardcore anti-capitalist activists, however, *Debt* receives glowing praise. The book allows the reader to step outside the boundaries of traditional economic thought, and instead ask questions about the system as a whole. While questioning the capitalist system is an activity as old as capitalism itself, *Debt* makes the exercise more accessible to today's audience. In a time of global

> **❝** Graeber … has emerged as perhaps the most influential radical political thinker of the moment. **❞**
> Kelefa Sanneh, *The New Yorker*

economic turmoil caused by personal and national debt, Graeber's book offers both sympathy and defiance.

Interaction

The first translation of *Debt* was published in Germany, which, as the primary creditor of the European debt crisis,* is often thought to occupy the moral high ground. While Graeber thinks of debt as a social invention that is often used to take advantage of others, German thinkers tend to view debt as a moral absolute. In *Debt*, Graeber notes that the German word for "debt," *schuld*, is also the word for "guilt." "But at the same time they realize that [debt is] about to destroy the European Union,* which is the last thing they want." *Debt* was a best seller for 11 weeks in Germany, indicating that Graeber's ideas may be gaining acceptance there. German voters, it might appear, are increasingly willing to at least discuss compromising with debtor nations.

If *Debt* can be said to argue against a specific group of people, it is the central bankers and policymakers who are responsible for resolving today's economic crises. The book's success in Germany, where a leading conservative politician praised it on the cover of the major daily *Frankfurter Allgemeine Zeitung*,[1] shows that policymakers might be following the citizens they serve in acknowledging the book's arguments.

The Continuing Debate

Graeber's has had some success in challenging policymakers through *Debt*. The chief research economist of the International Monetary

Fund* reached out to Graeber to discuss potential avenues for banking reform.[2] On the global economic policy-making elite, Graeber has said: "While they're telling everyone, 'Nothing to see here, carry on, carry on,' in fact those guys are panicking like crazy. You can see all these clear struggles going on where we don't really know what is at stake."[3] Graeber points out that even within the US Federal Reserve,* the central bank of the United States, a growing number of people advocate debt relief in the form of mortgage cancellation.[4] Of course, it is difficult to link global economic policy outcomes directly with the writing in *Debt* beyond Graeber's own accounts, as no policy paper from a global economic institution has yet cited *Debt* in its sources.

According to Graeber, there are "titanic struggles" occurring between those who want radical change and those who do not, but the lack of any progress boils down to inertia. While fundamental change may not occur, there is an increasing amount of sympathy for debt relief in the European debt crisis. "Looking back on this moment, we know the debt will be cancelled," Graeber has said. "Among those taking a long-term perspective, everyone agrees on that."[5]

NOTES

1 "Melville House Press Release: *Debt: The First 5,000 Years*," November 27, 2012, http://cdn.mhpbooks.com/2012/12/Debt-PR.pdf.

2 Hannah Chadeayne Appel, "Finance Is Just Another Word for Other People's Debts: An Interview with David Graeber," *Radical History Review*, no. 118 (2014): 171.

3 Appel, "Other People's Debts," 171.

4 Appel, "Other People's Debts," 171.

5 Appel, "Other People's Debts," 173.

WHERE NEXT?

KEY POINTS

- *Debt* will be remembered as an important book for anthropologists* because of its ability to spark a debate in economics* and economic history* using anthropological theory and evidence.

- Outside of academia, *Debt* is well positioned to have some influence in policy debates because it is accessible to a popular audience.

- *Debt* offers an immensely detailed, far-reaching, and critical discussion of some of the most fundamental institutions and ideas of capitalism.*

Potential

In terms of style and structure, *Debt: The First 5,000 Years* resembles both a history book and a declaration of belief. Debt also challenges the assumptions we have made over the last several hundred years about civilization, history, and society. While it provides an alternate view of history, *Debt* offers almost nothing to replace the policy assumptions that it challenges. Instead, the book serves as a giant signpost pointing the public and the intellectual community in a direction that may be anarchist* or reformist, but is essentially unknown.

The book will likely be remembered as a classic in anthropology for its ability to unite the reflections and observations of anthropologists on economic life and collectively aim them toward a common mission. However, pure economists have proven so unwilling to break free from rigid ideas like the Myth of the Barter* that Debt will probably remain out of the mainstream, on secondary reading lists as an object of curiosity.

> **"** You know radical change is coming when they call an anthropologist. **"**
>
> David Graeber, *Radical History Review*

Future Directions

Debt charts a new course for those within academia who are interested in alternatives to the traditional understanding of economic history. The book argues that anthropological study, rather than the legacy of the economist Adam Smith,* is the best way to engage with and interpret economic history. Anthropology has offered rich scholarship in "economic anthropology" since the writings of the pioneering sociologist Marcel Mauss* in the nineteenth century, but until Debt the insights have not been accessible to non-anthropologists. Because of this, the book makes way for an interdisciplinary* academic tradition—a tradition drawing on the aims and methods of different academic disciplines—that can develop a more thorough understanding of money and markets.*

It remains to be seen whether new, cross-discipline scholarship will translate into policy prescriptions. Economists have dominated policy making for nearly three centuries, and while heterodox* ideas—ideas outside of the mainstream—have been around in economics for more than a century, they remain on the fringes despite evidence that may support their claims.

Graeber's book and the ongoing economic climate imply that the various arguments against capitalism may be converging and getting stronger. David Graeber was invited to play an intellectual leadership role in Occupy Wall Street.* In the midst of the Syrian Civil War* (a conflict in the Middle East fought between those loyal to the Syrian President Assad and the rebel militias opposed to his rule), the Kurdish breakaway region of Rojava* has already formally rejected capitalism, taken steps to return to the "human economies" Graeber writes about in *Debt*, and hosted Graeber himself to see anarchist ideas in action.[1]

Summary

David Graeber's Debt is a vast work, more than 500 pages, on the origins and meaning of debt and money in human society. Published in the wake of the 2008 global financial crisis,* the book's sharp criticism of many of the foundational principles of capitalism has found an audience. *Debt's* central lesson is that the traditional understanding of economics and economic history has hidden the real story of capitalism, which is that money and debt allow the powerful to take advantage of the weak. War and slavery, Graeber argues, were instrumental in creating and shaping the institutions that form our modern market economy.

Debt uses anthropological and historical evidence to argue that money did not arise from a natural human tendency toward bartering,* despite the claims of Adam Smith and the economists that followed him. In fact, rather than base their lives on cutting deals with or profiting off of one another, Graeber argues that pre-market and non-market societies operated in the "human economy." People worked together to meet their needs based on complex networks of social obligations shaped by their personal relationships, and any barter-like behavior was for strangers who lacked mutual trust.

As rulers and states grew more powerful, however, social obligations gradually converted into measurable, impersonal debts, which disrupted human relationships. Graeber describes money as the tool used to calculate debts and justify punishments for those who owed them. With five millennia of history as evidence, Graeber argues that the commercial economy does not reflect human nature, and that it creates complex ways for the wealthy to take advantage of the poor. His book declares that capitalism itself is far from the fair and equitable system many imagine, and that capitalism can be undone.

NOTES

1   David Graeber, "Why Is the World Ignoring the Revolutionary Kurds in Syria?" *Guardian*, October 8, 2014, http://www.theguardian.com/commentisfree/2014/oct/08/why-world-ignoring-revolutionary-kurds-syria-isis.

GLOSSARY

GLOSSARY OF TERMS

Anarchism: a political philosophy advocating the destruction of governments in favor of stateless societies.

Anthropology: the academic study of humanity and human society.

Austerity: a set of economic policies intended to reduce government budget deficits and the national debt by cutting government spending and paying back loans.

Austrian School: a school of economic thought that focuses on the rationality and actions of individuals as the primary forces in an economy.

Axial Age: a period of ancient history characterized by great advances in human philosophical thought, normally considered as being 800 B.C.E.–200 B.C.E. (although defined by David Graeber as 800 B.C.E.–600 C.E.).

Barter: the practice of trading goods or services directly for other goods or services, without exchanging money. Barter is possible only when each party has something that the other wants.

Brahmanas: a collection of ancient Indian religious scriptures including myths, legends, explanations of rituals, and philosophy accompanying older scriptures known as the Vedas.

Capitalism: an economic system in which trade, production, and property are largely or entirely in the hands of private individuals or corporations.

Chartalism: the economic school of thought that teaches that money arose from states' efforts to direct market activity rather than spontaneously to enable barter.

Colonialism: the forced acquisition, settlement, and political or economic control of one territory by the political power of another territory.

Commodity: an object that can be traded, bought, or sold.

Communism: a political ideology advocating common ownership of the means of production and the destruction of social relationship structures.

Credit: the ability to purchase goods or services without immediate payment, based on the seller's trust that payment will be received at a later time.

Credit theory of money: a collection of economic schools of thought that teach that money is essentially a form of credit and debt.

Debt crisis of the 1980s: a debt crisis triggered by unregulated lending from global banks to governments in developing countries that borrowed (and sometimes wasted) more money than they could repay. In response, global trade and development organizations (the International Monetary Fund and the World Bank) forced changes that created hardships for those people in developing countries who benefitted from public welfare programs and local jobs.

Debt restructuring: a process in which a debtor is allowed to renegotiate the terms or to reduce the value of repayment for outstanding debt.

Developing country: a sovereign state with an underdeveloped industrial base and a low quality of life relative to other states.

Economic history: a discipline of the social sciences that studies the history and development of economies.

Economics: a discipline of the social sciences that studies human behavior and social systems under conditions of scarce means and unlimited wants.

The Economist: an English-language weekly magazine covering political and economic affairs, established in London in 1843.

Ethnography: a sub-discipline within anthropology concerned with the systematic study and graphical representation of human cultures.

Eurasia: the combined landmass encompassing the continents of Europe and Asia.

European debt crisis: an ongoing debt crisis within the European Union in which several member states have been unable to repay loans to private and public creditors.

European Union: a political and economic union of 28 European nations.

Federal Reserve: the central bank of the United States of America.

Fulbright Fellowship: a highly competitive scholarship offering American students and scholars funding to conduct research or studies overseas.

Geography: an academic discipline concerned with the study of the physical features of the earth and its relationship with human activity.

Global financial crisis of 2008: the most serious financial crisis since the Great Depression of the 1930s. The crisis was caused by the collapse of the American housing bubble and resulted in mass defaults on debts, affecting financial institutions and markets worldwide.

Global justice movement: a network of international social activist movements that oppose corporate globalization.

Globalization: the process of increasing interconnectedness among global markets, politics, and cultures.

Gold standard: a monetary system in which the value of the standard currency is based on a fixed quantity of gold.

Heterodox economics: theories, practices, and schools of thought within economics that exist outside of the mainstream teachings of the discipline.

Inflation: an increase in prices and fall in the purchasing power of money within an economy.

Interdisciplinary: drawing on the aims and methods of different academic disciplines.

International Monetary Fund (IMF): an international organization created in 1944 to foster global monetary cooperation by assisting international trade and providing help in financial or monetary crises.

Keynesian economics: an economic school of thought that teaches that in the short run a country's economic output is influenced by the economy's level of total demand.

London School of Economics: a British public research university focused on the study of the social sciences, founded in London in 1895.

Market: an economic system in which parties buy and sell goods and services.

Mesopotamia: the name for the area of the Middle East, much of it in Iraq, lying between the Tigris and Euphrates rivers. The region is generally considered to be the home of the earliest human civilizations.

Myth of Barter: the idea that money arose spontaneously as a solution to the inconveniences of barter. Economists have believed this for centuries, but many anthropologists argue that it is not correct.

1979 energy crisis: an economic event that occurred in the United States in which there was a panic about shortage of the supply of oil as a result of political upheaval in Iran, leading to sharply increased prices.

Occupy Wall Street (OWS): a global protest movement against economic and social inequality started in 2011 in response to the 2008 global financial crisis.

Path dependency: a theory within the disciplines of development studies and economic history that asserts that states develop based on predetermined factors, such as geography or prior history.

Political economy: the study of economics in relation to politics.

Politics: an academic discipline concerned with the study of governance, power relations, and the state.

Primordial debt: a theory among some sociologists, historians, and economists that government taxes are an extension of ancient ideas of debt to society, the gods, or the cosmos.

Progressive tax: taxation where the tax rate increases as income increases.

Rentier: a person or institution living on profits from capital, such as property or investments.

Revolution: the overthrow of a given system of governance or authority, usually by forcible means.

Rojava: a breakaway Kurdish proto-state in northern Syria.

Socratic: eliciting truth in an argument through the practice of question and answer.

Spanish Civil War: a civil war fought in Spain between 1936 and 1939 between loyalists to the Second Spanish Republic and supporters of General Francisco Franco.

Spanish Revolution: a social revolution in Spain in 1936 that led to the widespread implementation of anarchist principles in various parts of the country during the Spanish Civil War.

Syrian Civil War: an ongoing civil war in Syria between the national government and various rebel movements.

Union: an organization of traders, workers, or laborers who join together to negotiate for better salaries or working conditions.

World Bank: an international organization headquartered in Geneva that provides loans to developing countries for capital projects.

World Trade Organization (WTO): an intergovernmental organization headquartered in Washington, DC, that regulates global trade by establishing trade laws and systems for settling disputes.

Young Communist League: an activist organization with chapters around the world, dedicated to promoting communism and Marxist thought among young people.

PEOPLE MENTIONED IN THE TEXT

Aristotle (384–322 B.C.E.) was a Greek philosopher and scientist. He was the first person known to theorize on the origins of money, claiming that it arose spontaneously as a solution to the inconveniences of barter.

Mike Beggs is a lecturer in political economy at the University of Sydney.

Maurice Bloch (b. 1939) is a British anthropologist and professor at the London School of Economics.

Jared Diamond (b. 1937) is an American scientist and geographer. His ideas on the path dependency of nations brought influence from the fields of anthropology and geography to economic history.

Francisco Franco (1892–1975) was a Spanish general; following the removal of the Spanish monarchy in 1931, and the election of a socialist government in 1936, he participated in a coup that started the Spanish Civil War. He subsequently became head of state and ruled as a right-wing dictator.

Michael Hardt (b. 1960) is an American political philosopher. His writings on class oppression and globalization have drawn on Graeber's work regarding debt.

Keith Hart (b. 1943) is a British economic anthropologist. He was a pioneer in the development of the idea of the "human economy" and argued that money is simultaneously both a form of credit and a commodity.

Caroline Humphrey (b. 1943) is a British anthropologist. She has investigated the role of barter in human society extensively and has found that there is no evidence to support the theory that barter preceded the creation of money.

Georg Friedrich Knapp (1842–1926) was a German economist. He was the founder of the Chartalist school of monetary theory.

Paul Krugman (b. 1953) is a Nobel Prize-winning American economist. He is a prominent supporter of Keynesian economics and an opponent of austerity.

Karl Marx (1818–83) was a Prussian political philosopher and economist. He was the founder of Marxism and argued that human societies progress through class struggle, especially in *Capital*.

J. W. Mason is an assistant professor of economics at John Jay College, City University of New York.

Marcel Mauss (1872–1950) was a French sociologist. He is considered a pioneer in the discipline of anthropology and is particularly known for his theories on gift exchange.

Carl Menger (1840–1921) was an Austrian economist. He was the founder of the Austrian School of economic thought.

Alfred Mitchell-Innes (1864–1950) was a British economist. He was a proponent of the credit theory of money.

Antonio Negri (b. 1933) is an Italian Marxist political philosopher. He is a prominent figure in anti-capitalist activist movements.

Thomas Piketty (b. 1971) is a French economist. He is best known for his work highlighting the propensity of unrestricted capitalism to result in economic and social inequality.

Karl Polanyi (1886–1964) was a Hungarian American economic historian. He was a prominent opponent of traditional economic history narratives and argued that markets were created and engineered by the state.

Carmen Reinhart (b. 1955) is a Cuban American economist. She argued in favor of austerity measures in response to the 2008 global financial crisis together with Kenneth Rogoff.

Dani Rodrik (b. 1957) is a Turkish economist and professor at Harvard University. He is known for his work in development economics.

Kenneth Rogoff (b. 1953) is an American economist. He argued in favor of austerity measures in response to the 2008 global financial crisis together with Carmen Reinhart.

Amartya Sen (b. 1933) is a Bangladeshi economist. He is best known for his work on poverty relief and development economics, and has strongly opposed austerity measures in response to debt crises.

Adam Smith (1723–90) was a Scottish philosopher and political economist. He is considered the father of the discipline of economics, having written its first major work, *The Wealth of Nations*.

Noah Smith is an assistant professor of finance at Stony Brook University.

Socrates (469 B.C.E.–399 B.C.E.) was a philosopher in ancient Greece, and considered one of the founders of Western philosophy. He is most known for his development of the Socratic method, which involves learning through critical discussion.

Joseph Stieglitz (b. 1943) is an American economist and professor at Columbia University. He was chief economist of the World Bank from 1997 to 2000.

WORKS CITED

WORKS CITED

Appel, Hannah Chadeayne. "Finance Is Just Another Word for Other People's Debts: An Interview with David Graeber." *Radical History Review*, no. 118 (2014): 168–73.

Barker, T. C. "The Beginnings of the Economic History Society." *The Economic History Review* 30, no. 1 (February, 1977): 1–19.

Beggs, Mike. "Debt: The First 500 Pages." *Jacobin*, August, 2012. Accessed September 25, 2015. https://www.jacobinmag.com/2012/08/debt-the-first-500-pages/.

———. "On Debt: A Reply to Josh Mason." *Jacobin*, September 20, 2012. Accessed September 25, 2015. https://www.jacobinmag.com/2012/09/on-debt-a-reply-to-josh-mason/.

Bloch, Maurice. "Letter from Maurice Bloch, London School of Economics" (2005). Accessed September 25, 2015. http://www.geocities.ws/graebersolidarity/blochletter.html.

Graeber, David. "Can We Still Write Big Question Sorts of Books?" *Savage Minds*, July 31, 2011. Accessed September 13, 2015. http://savageminds.org/2011/07/31/can-we-still-write-big-question-sorts-of-books/.

———. *Debt: The First 5,000 Years*. Brooklyn, NY: Melville House.

———. *Fragments of an Anarchist Anthropology*. Chicago: Prickly Paradigm Press, 2004.

———. *Lost People: Magic and the Legacy of Slavery in Madagascar*. Bloomington, IN: Indiana University Press, 2007.

———. "Savage Capitalism Is Back—And It Will Not Tame Itself." *Guardian*, May 30, 2014. Accessed September 19, 2015. http://www.theguardian.com/commentisfree/2014/may/30/savage-capitalism-back-radical-challenge.

———. *Toward an Anthropological Theory of Value: The False Coin of Our Own Dreams*. New York: Palgrave Macmillan, 2001.

———. "Why Is the World Ignoring the Revolutionary Kurds in Syria?" *Guardian*, October 8, 2014. Accessed September 21, 2015. http://www.theguardian.com/commentisfree/2014/oct/08/why-world-ignoring-revolutionary-kurds-syria-isis.

Graeber, David, and Thomas Piketty. "Soak the Rich: An Exchange on Capital, Debt, and the Future." *The Baffler*, July 31, 2014. Accessed September 18, 2015. http://thebaffler.com/odds-and-ends/soak-the-rich.

Hart, Keith. "Heads or Tails? Two Sides of the Coin." *Man* 21, no. 4 (December, 1986): 637–56.

———. "In Rousseau's Footsteps: David Graeber and the Anthropology of Unequal Society." *The Memory Bank*, July 4, 2012. Accessed September 19, 2015. http://thememorybank.co.uk/2012/07/04/in-rousseaus-footsteps-david-graeber-and-the-anthropology-of-unequal-society-2/.

Humphrey, Caroline. "Barter and Economic Disintegration." *Man* 20, no. 1 (March, 1985): 48–72.

Jeffries, Stuart. "David Graeber Interview: 'So Many People Spend Their Working Lives Doing Jobs They Think Are Unnecessary.'" *Guardian*, March 21, 2015. Accessed September 23, 2015. http://www.theguardian.com/books/2015/mar/21/books-interview-david-graeber-the-utopia-of-rules.

Karimzadi, Shahzavar. *Money and Its Origins*. Abingdon: Routledge, 2013.

Keynes, John Maynard. *A Treatise on Money*. New York: Harcourt, Brace, & Co, 1930.

Knapp, Georg Friedrich. *The State Theory of Money*. London: Macmillan & Company, 1924.

Marx, Karl. *Das Kapital*. Chicago: Charles H. Kerr & Co., 1906.

Mason, J. W. "In Defense of David Graeber's Debt." *Jacobin*, September 18, 2012. Accessed September 23, 2015. https://www.jacobinmag.com/2012/09/in-defense-of-david-graebers-debt/.

Maurer, Bill. "David Graeber's Wunderkammer, *Debt: The First 5,000 Years*." *Anthropological Forum* 23, no. 1 (2013): 79–93.

Mauss, Marcel. *The Gift*. London: Cohen & West, 1954.

Meaney, Thomas. "Anarchist Anthropology." *New York Times*, December 8, 2011. Accessed September 21, 2015. http://www.nytimes.com/2011/12/11/books/review/anarchist-anthropology.html.

Melville House Publishers. "Melville House Press Release: *Debt: The First 5,000 Years*." November 27, 2012. Accessed September 21, 2015. http://cdn.mhpbooks.com/2012/12/Debt-PR.pdf.

Mitchell Innes, Alfred. "The Credit Theory of Money." *The Banking Journal* 31 (1914): 151–68.

———. "What is Money?" *The Banking Journal* 30 (1913): 377–408.

Negri, Antonio, and Michael Hardt. *Declaration*. New York: Argo-Navis, 2012.

Peden, Knox. "The Abstractions of History." *The Sydney Review of Books*, July 22, 2014. Accessed September 18, 2015. http://www.sydneyreviewofbooks.

com/capital-twenty-first-century-thomas-piketty/.

Piketty, Thomas, and Arthur Goldhammer. *Capital in the Twenty-First Century*. Cambridge, MA: The Belknap Press of Harvard University Press, 2014.

Polanyi, Karl. *The Great Transformation*. Boston: Beacon Press, 1944.

Reinhart, Carmen M., and Kenneth S. Rogoff. "Growth in a Time of Debt." *American Economic Review* 100, no. 2 (May, 2010): 573–8.

Runciman, David. "*The Democracy Project: A History, a Crisis, a Movement* by David Graeber – Review." *Guardian*, March 28, 2013. Accessed September 21, 2015. http://www.theguardian.com/books/2013/mar/28/democracy-project-david-graeber-review.

Sanneh, Kelefa. "Paint Bombs: David Graeber's 'The Democracy Project' and the Anarchist Revival." *The New Yorker*, May 13, 2013. Accessed September 23, 2015. http://www.newyorker.com/magazine/2013/05/13/paint-bombs.

Schalliol, Gavin. "Thomas Piketty: 'Germany Has Never Repaid Its Debts. It Has No Right to Lecture Greece.'" *The Wire*, July 8, 2015. Accessed September 23, 2015. http://thewire.in/2015/07/08/thomas-piketty-germany-has-never-repaid-its-debts-it-has-no-right-to-lecture-greece-5851/.

Sen, Amartya. "The Economic Consequences of Austerity." *The New Statesman*, 4 June 2015.

Smith, Noah. "David Graeber: Debt Is Bad, or Something…?" *Noahpinion*, February 13, 2013. Accessed September 18, 2015. http://noahpinionblog.blogspot.co.uk/2013/02/david-graeber-debt-is-bad-or-something.html.

THE MACAT LIBRARY
BY DISCIPLINE

The Macat Library By Discipline

AFRICANA STUDIES

Chinua Achebe's *An Image of Africa: Racism in Conrad's Heart of Darkness*
W. E. B. Du Bois's *The Souls of Black Folk*
Zora Neale Huston's *Characteristics of Negro Expression*
Martin Luther King Jr's *Why We Can't Wait*
Toni Morrison's *Playing in the Dark: Whiteness in the American Literary Imagination*

ANTHROPOLOGY

Arjun Appadurai's *Modernity at Large: Cultural Dimensions of Globalisation*
Philippe Ariès's *Centuries of Childhood*
Franz Boas's *Race, Language and Culture*
Kim Chan & Renée Mauborgne's *Blue Ocean Strategy*
Jared Diamond's *Guns, Germs & Steel: the Fate of Human Societies*
Jared Diamond's *Collapse: How Societies Choose to Fail or Survive*
E. E. Evans-Pritchard's *Witchcraft, Oracles and Magic Among the Azande*
James Ferguson's *The Anti-Politics Machine*
Clifford Geertz's *The Interpretation of Cultures*
David Graeber's *Debt: the First 5000 Years*
Karen Ho's *Liquidated: An Ethnography of Wall Street*
Geert Hofstede's *Culture's Consequences: Comparing Values, Behaviors, Institutes and Organizations across Nations*
Claude Lévi-Strauss's *Structural Anthropology*
Jay Macleod's *Ain't No Makin' It: Aspirations and Attainment in a Low-Income Neighborhood*
Saba Mahmood's *The Politics of Piety: The Islamic Revival and the Feminist Subject*
Marcel Mauss's *The Gift*

BUSINESS

Jean Lave & Etienne Wenger's *Situated Learning*
Theodore Levitt's *Marketing Myopia*
Burton G. Malkiel's *A Random Walk Down Wall Street*
Douglas McGregor's *The Human Side of Enterprise*
Michael Porter's *Competitive Strategy: Creating and Sustaining Superior Performance*
John Kotter's *Leading Change*
C. K. Prahalad & Gary Hamel's *The Core Competence of the Corporation*

CRIMINOLOGY

Michelle Alexander's *The New Jim Crow: Mass Incarceration in the Age of Colorblindness*
Michael R. Gottfredson & Travis Hirschi's *A General Theory of Crime*
Richard Herrnstein & Charles A. Murray's *The Bell Curve: Intelligence and Class Structure in American Life*
Elizabeth Loftus's *Eyewitness Testimony*
Jay Macleod's *Ain't No Makin' It: Aspirations and Attainment in a Low-Income Neighborhood*
Philip Zimbardo's *The Lucifer Effect*

ECONOMICS

Janet Abu-Lughod's *Before European Hegemony*
Ha-Joon Chang's *Kicking Away the Ladder*
David Brion Davis's *The Problem of Slavery in the Age of Revolution*
Milton Friedman's *The Role of Monetary Policy*
Milton Friedman's *Capitalism and Freedom*
David Graeber's *Debt: the First 5000 Years*
Friedrich Hayek's *The Road to Serfdom*
Karen Ho's *Liquidated: An Ethnography of Wall Street*

John Maynard Keynes's *The General Theory of Employment, Interest and Money*
Charles P. Kindleberger's *Manias, Panics and Crashes*
Robert Lucas's *Why Doesn't Capital Flow from Rich to Poor Countries?*
Burton G. Malkiel's *A Random Walk Down Wall Street*
Thomas Robert Malthus's *An Essay on the Principle of Population*
Karl Marx's *Capital*
Thomas Piketty's *Capital in the Twenty-First Century*
Amartya Sen's *Development as Freedom*
Adam Smith's *The Wealth of Nations*
Nassim Nicholas Taleb's *The Black Swan: The Impact of the Highly Improbable*
Amos Tversky's & Daniel Kahneman's *Judgment under Uncertainty: Heuristics and Biases*
Mahbub Ul Haq's *Reflections on Human Development*
Max Weber's *The Protestant Ethic and the Spirit of Capitalism*

FEMINISM AND GENDER STUDIES

Judith Butler's *Gender Trouble*
Simone De Beauvoir's *The Second Sex*
Michel Foucault's *History of Sexuality*
Betty Friedan's *The Feminine Mystique*
Saba Mahmood's *The Politics of Piety: The Islamic Revival and the Feminist Subject*
Joan Wallach Scott's *Gender and the Politics of History*
Mary Wollstonecraft's *A Vindication of the Rights of Woman*
Virginia Woolf's *A Room of One's Own*

GEOGRAPHY

The Brundtland Report's *Our Common Future*
Rachel Carson's *Silent Spring*
Charles Darwin's *On the Origin of Species*
James Ferguson's *The Anti-Politics Machine*
Jane Jacobs's *The Death and Life of Great American Cities*
James Lovelock's *Gaia: A New Look at Life on Earth*
Amartya Sen's *Development as Freedom*
Mathis Wackernagel & William Rees's *Our Ecological Footprint*

HISTORY

Janet Abu-Lughod's *Before European Hegemony*
Benedict Anderson's *Imagined Communities*
Bernard Bailyn's *The Ideological Origins of the American Revolution*
Hanna Batatu's *The Old Social Classes And The Revolutionary Movements Of Iraq*
Christopher Browning's *Ordinary Men: Reserve Police Batallion 101 and the Final Solution in Poland*
Edmund Burke's *Reflections on the Revolution in France*
William Cronon's *Nature's Metropolis: Chicago And The Great West*
Alfred W. Crosby's *The Columbian Exchange*
Hamid Dabashi's *Iran: A People Interrupted*
David Brion Davis's *The Problem of Slavery in the Age of Revolution*
Nathalie Zemon Davis's *The Return of Martin Guerre*
Jared Diamond's *Guns, Germs & Steel: the Fate of Human Societies*
Frank Dikotter's *Mao's Great Famine*
John W Dower's *War Without Mercy: Race And Power In The Pacific War*
W. E. B. Du Bois's *The Souls of Black Folk*
Richard J. Evans's *In Defence of History*
Lucien Febvre's *The Problem of Unbelief in the 16th Century*
Sheila Fitzpatrick's *Everyday Stalinism*

The Macat Library By Discipline

Eric Foner's *Reconstruction: America's Unfinished Revolution, 1863-1877*
Michel Foucault's *Discipline and Punish*
Michel Foucault's *History of Sexuality*
Francis Fukuyama's *The End of History and the Last Man*
John Lewis Gaddis's *We Now Know: Rethinking Cold War History*
Ernest Gellner's *Nations and Nationalism*
Eugene Genovese's *Roll, Jordan, Roll: The World the Slaves Made*
Carlo Ginzburg's *The Night Battles*
Daniel Goldhagen's *Hitler's Willing Executioners*
Jack Goldstone's *Revolution and Rebellion in the Early Modern World*
Antonio Gramsci's *The Prison Notebooks*
Alexander Hamilton, John Jay & James Madison's *The Federalist Papers*
Christopher Hill's *The World Turned Upside Down*
Carole Hillenbrand's *The Crusades: Islamic Perspectives*
Thomas Hobbes's *Leviathan*
Eric Hobsbawm's *The Age Of Revolution*
John A. Hobson's *Imperialism: A Study*
Albert Hourani's *History of the Arab Peoples*
Samuel P. Huntington's *The Clash of Civilizations and the Remaking of World Order*
C. L. R. James's *The Black Jacobins*
Tony Judt's *Postwar: A History of Europe Since 1945*
Ernst Kantorowicz's *The King's Two Bodies: A Study in Medieval Political Theology*
Paul Kennedy's *The Rise and Fall of the Great Powers*
Ian Kershaw's *The "Hitler Myth": Image and Reality in the Third Reich*
John Maynard Keynes's *The General Theory of Employment, Interest and Money*
Charles P. Kindleberger's *Manias, Panics and Crashes*
Martin Luther King Jr's *Why We Can't Wait*
Henry Kissinger's *World Order: Reflections on the Character of Nations and the Course of History*
Thomas Kuhn's *The Structure of Scientific Revolutions*
Georges Lefebvre's *The Coming of the French Revolution*
John Locke's *Two Treatises of Government*
Niccolò Machiavelli's *The Prince*
Thomas Robert Malthus's *An Essay on the Principle of Population*
Mahmood Mamdani's *Citizen and Subject: Contemporary Africa And The Legacy Of Late Colonialism*
Karl Marx's *Capital*
Stanley Milgram's *Obedience to Authority*
John Stuart Mill's *On Liberty*
Thomas Paine's *Common Sense*
Thomas Paine's *Rights of Man*
Geoffrey Parker's *Global Crisis: War, Climate Change and Catastrophe in the Seventeenth Century*
Jonathan Riley-Smith's *The First Crusade and the Idea of Crusading*
Jean-Jacques Rousseau's *The Social Contract*
Joan Wallach Scott's *Gender and the Politics of History*
Theda Skocpol's *States and Social Revolutions*
Adam Smith's *The Wealth of Nations*
Timothy Snyder's *Bloodlands: Europe Between Hitler and Stalin*
Sun Tzu's *The Art of War*
Keith Thomas's *Religion and the Decline of Magic*
Thucydides's *The History of the Peloponnesian War*
Frederick Jackson Turner's *The Significance of the Frontier in American History*
Odd Arne Westad's *The Global Cold War: Third World Interventions And The Making Of Our Times*

LITERATURE

Chinua Achebe's *An Image of Africa: Racism in Conrad's Heart of Darkness*
Roland Barthes's *Mythologies*
Homi K. Bhabha's *The Location of Culture*
Judith Butler's *Gender Trouble*
Simone De Beauvoir's *The Second Sex*
Ferdinand De Saussure's *Course in General Linguistics*
T. S. Eliot's *The Sacred Wood: Essays on Poetry and Criticism*
Zora Neale Huston's *Characteristics of Negro Expression*
Toni Morrison's *Playing in the Dark: Whiteness in the American Literary Imagination*
Edward Said's *Orientalism*
Gayatri Chakravorty Spivak's *Can the Subaltern Speak?*
Mary Wollstonecraft's *A Vindication of the Rights of Women*
Virginia Woolf's *A Room of One's Own*

PHILOSOPHY

Elizabeth Anscombe's *Modern Moral Philosophy*
Hannah Arendt's *The Human Condition*
Aristotle's *Metaphysics*
Aristotle's *Nicomachean Ethics*
Edmund Gettier's *Is Justified True Belief Knowledge?*
Georg Wilhelm Friedrich Hegel's *Phenomenology of Spirit*
David Hume's *Dialogues Concerning Natural Religion*
David Hume's *The Enquiry for Human Understanding*
Immanuel Kant's *Religion within the Boundaries of Mere Reason*
Immanuel Kant's *Critique of Pure Reason*
Søren Kierkegaard's *The Sickness Unto Death*
Søren Kierkegaard's *Fear and Trembling*
C. S. Lewis's *The Abolition of Man*
Alasdair MacIntyre's *After Virtue*
Marcus Aurelius's *Meditations*
Friedrich Nietzsche's *On the Genealogy of Morality*
Friedrich Nietzsche's *Beyond Good and Evil*
Plato's *Republic*
Plato's *Symposium*
Jean-Jacques Rousseau's *The Social Contract*
Gilbert Ryle's *The Concept of Mind*
Baruch Spinoza's *Ethics*
Sun Tzu's *The Art of War*
Ludwig Wittgenstein's *Philosophical Investigations*

POLITICS

Benedict Anderson's *Imagined Communities*
Aristotle's *Politics*
Bernard Bailyn's *The Ideological Origins of the American Revolution*
Edmund Burke's *Reflections on the Revolution in France*
John C. Calhoun's *A Disquisition on Government*
Ha-Joon Chang's *Kicking Away the Ladder*
Hamid Dabashi's *Iran: A People Interrupted*
Hamid Dabashi's *Theology of Discontent: The Ideological Foundation of the Islamic Revolution in Iran*
Robert Dahl's *Democracy and its Critics*
Robert Dahl's *Who Governs?*
David Brion Davis's *The Problem of Slavery in the Age of Revolution*

The Macat Library By Discipline

Alexis De Tocqueville's *Democracy in America*
James Ferguson's *The Anti-Politics Machine*
Frank Dikotter's *Mao's Great Famine*
Sheila Fitzpatrick's *Everyday Stalinism*
Eric Foner's *Reconstruction: America's Unfinished Revolution, 1863-1877*
Milton Friedman's *Capitalism and Freedom*
Francis Fukuyama's *The End of History and the Last Man*
John Lewis Gaddis's *We Now Know: Rethinking Cold War History*
Ernest Gellner's *Nations and Nationalism*
David Graeber's *Debt: the First 5000 Years*
Antonio Gramsci's *The Prison Notebooks*
Alexander Hamilton, John Jay & James Madison's *The Federalist Papers*
Friedrich Hayek's *The Road to Serfdom*
Christopher Hill's *The World Turned Upside Down*
Thomas Hobbes's *Leviathan*
John A. Hobson's *Imperialism: A Study*
Samuel P. Huntington's *The Clash of Civilizations and the Remaking of World Order*
Tony Judt's *Postwar: A History of Europe Since 1945*
David C. Kang's *China Rising: Peace, Power and Order in East Asia*
Paul Kennedy's *The Rise and Fall of Great Powers*
Robert Keohane's *After Hegemony*
Martin Luther King Jr.'s *Why We Can't Wait*
Henry Kissinger's *World Order: Reflections on the Character of Nations and the Course of History*
John Locke's *Two Treatises of Government*
Niccolò Machiavelli's *The Prince*
Thomas Robert Malthus's *An Essay on the Principle of Population*
Mahmood Mamdani's *Citizen and Subject: Contemporary Africa And The Legacy Of Late Colonialism*
Karl Marx's *Capital*
John Stuart Mill's *On Liberty*
John Stuart Mill's *Utilitarianism*
Hans Morgenthau's *Politics Among Nations*
Thomas Paine's *Common Sense*
Thomas Paine's *Rights of Man*
Thomas Piketty's *Capital in the Twenty-First Century*
Robert D. Putman's *Bowling Alone*
John Rawls's *Theory of Justice*
Jean-Jacques Rousseau's *The Social Contract*
Theda Skocpol's *States and Social Revolutions*
Adam Smith's *The Wealth of Nations*
Sun Tzu's *The Art of War*
Henry David Thoreau's *Civil Disobedience*
Thucydides's *The History of the Peloponnesian War*
Kenneth Waltz's *Theory of International Politics*
Max Weber's *Politics as a Vocation*
Odd Arne Westad's *The Global Cold War: Third World Interventions And The Making Of Our Times*

POSTCOLONIAL STUDIES

Roland Barthes's *Mythologies*
Frantz Fanon's *Black Skin, White Masks*
Homi K. Bhabha's *The Location of Culture*
Gustavo Gutiérrez's *A Theology of Liberation*
Edward Said's *Orientalism*
Gayatri Chakravorty Spivak's *Can the Subaltern Speak?*

PSYCHOLOGY

Gordon Allport's *The Nature of Prejudice*
Alan Baddeley & Graham Hitch's *Aggression: A Social Learning Analysis*
Albert Bandura's *Aggression: A Social Learning Analysis*
Leon Festinger's *A Theory of Cognitive Dissonance*
Sigmund Freud's *The Interpretation of Dreams*
Betty Friedan's *The Feminine Mystique*
Michael R. Gottfredson & Travis Hirschi's *A General Theory of Crime*
Eric Hoffer's *The True Believer: Thoughts on the Nature of Mass Movements*
William James's *Principles of Psychology*
Elizabeth Loftus's *Eyewitness Testimony*
A. H. Maslow's *A Theory of Human Motivation*
Stanley Milgram's *Obedience to Authority*
Steven Pinker's *The Better Angels of Our Nature*
Oliver Sacks's *The Man Who Mistook His Wife For a Hat*
Richard Thaler & Cass Sunstein's *Nudge: Improving Decisions About Health, Wealth and Happiness*
Amos Tversky's *Judgment under Uncertainty: Heuristics and Biases*
Philip Zimbardo's *The Lucifer Effect*

SCIENCE

Rachel Carson's *Silent Spring*
William Cronon's *Nature's Metropolis: Chicago And The Great West*
Alfred W. Crosby's *The Columbian Exchange*
Charles Darwin's *On the Origin of Species*
Richard Dawkin's *The Selfish Gene*
Thomas Kuhn's *The Structure of Scientific Revolutions*
Geoffrey Parker's *Global Crisis: War, Climate Change and Catastrophe in the Seventeenth Century*
Mathis Wackernagel & William Rees's *Our Ecological Footprint*

SOCIOLOGY

Michelle Alexander's *The New Jim Crow: Mass Incarceration in the Age of Colorblindness*
Gordon Allport's *The Nature of Prejudice*
Albert Bandura's *Aggression: A Social Learning Analysis*
Hanna Batatu's *The Old Social Classes And The Revolutionary Movements Of Iraq*
Ha-Joon Chang's *Kicking Away the Ladder*
W. E. B. Du Bois's *The Souls of Black Folk*
Émile Durkheim's *On Suicide*
Frantz Fanon's *Black Skin, White Masks*
Frantz Fanon's *The Wretched of the Earth*
Eric Foner's *Reconstruction: America's Unfinished Revolution, 1863-1877*
Eugene Genovese's *Roll, Jordan, Roll: The World the Slaves Made*
Jack Goldstone's *Revolution and Rebellion in the Early Modern World*
Antonio Gramsci's *The Prison Notebooks*
Richard Herrnstein & Charles A Murray's *The Bell Curve: Intelligence and Class Structure in American Life*
Eric Hoffer's *The True Believer: Thoughts on the Nature of Mass Movements*
Jane Jacobs's *The Death and Life of Great American Cities*
Robert Lucas's *Why Doesn't Capital Flow from Rich to Poor Countries?*
Jay Macleod's *Ain't No Makin' It: Aspirations and Attainment in a Low Income Neighborhood*
Elaine May's *Homeward Bound: American Families in the Cold War Era*
Douglas McGregor's *The Human Side of Enterprise*
C. Wright Mills's *The Sociological Imagination*

The Macat Library By Discipline

Thomas Piketty's *Capital in the Twenty-First Century*
Robert D. Putman's *Bowling Alone*
David Riesman's *The Lonely Crowd: A Study of the Changing American Character*
Edward Said's *Orientalism*
Joan Wallach Scott's *Gender and the Politics of History*
Theda Skocpol's *States and Social Revolutions*
Max Weber's *The Protestant Ethic and the Spirit of Capitalism*

THEOLOGY

Augustine's *Confessions*
Benedict's *Rule of St Benedict*
Gustavo Gutiérrez's *A Theology of Liberation*
Carole Hillenbrand's *The Crusades: Islamic Perspectives*
David Hume's *Dialogues Concerning Natural Religion*
Immanuel Kant's *Religion within the Boundaries of Mere Reason*
Ernst Kantorowicz's *The King's Two Bodies: A Study in Medieval Political Theology*
Søren Kierkegaard's *The Sickness Unto Death*
C. S. Lewis's *The Abolition of Man*
Saba Mahmood's *The Politics of Piety: The Islamic Revival and the Feminist Subject*
Baruch Spinoza's *Ethics*
Keith Thomas's *Religion and the Decline of Magic*

COMING SOON

Chris Argyris's *The Individual and the Organisation*
Seyla Benhabib's *The Rights of Others*
Walter Benjamin's *The Work Of Art in the Age of Mechanical Reproduction*
John Berger's *Ways of Seeing*
Pierre Bourdieu's *Outline of a Theory of Practice*
Mary Douglas's *Purity and Danger*
Roland Dworkin's *Taking Rights Seriously*
James G. March's *Exploration and Exploitation in Organisational Learning*
Ikujiro Nonaka's *A Dynamic Theory of Organizational Knowledge Creation*
Griselda Pollock's *Vision and Difference*
Amartya Sen's *Inequality Re-Examined*
Susan Sontag's *On Photography*
Yasser Tabbaa's *The Transformation of Islamic Art*
Ludwig von Mises's *Theory of Money and Credit*

Macat Disciplines

Access the greatest ideas and thinkers across entire disciplines, including

AFRICANA STUDIES

Chinua Achebe's *An Image of Africa: Racism in Conrad's Heart of Darkness*

W. E. B. Du Bois's *The Souls of Black Folk*

Zora Neale Hurston's *Characteristics of Negro Expression*

Martin Luther King Jr.'s *Why We Can't Wait*

Toni Morrison's *Playing in the Dark: Whiteness in the American Literary Imagination*

Macat analyses are available from all good bookshops and libraries.

Access hundreds of analyses through one, multimedia tool.
Join free for one month **library.macat.com**

Macat Disciplines

Access the greatest ideas and thinkers across entire disciplines, including

FEMINISM, GENDER AND QUEER STUDIES

Simone De Beauvoir's
The Second Sex

Michel Foucault's
History of Sexuality

Betty Friedan's
The Feminine Mystique

Saba Mahmood's
*The Politics of Piety:
The Islamic Revival and
the Feminist Subject*

Joan Wallach Scott's
*Gender and the
Politics of History*

Mary Wollstonecraft's
*A Vindication of the
Rights of Woman*

Virginia Woolf's
A Room of One's Own

Judith Butler's
Gender Trouble

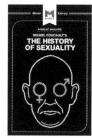

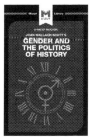

Macat analyses are available from all good bookshops and libraries.

Access hundreds of analyses through one, multimedia tool.
Join free for one month **library.macat.com**

Macat Disciplines

Access the greatest ideas and thinkers across entire disciplines, including

INEQUALITY

Ha-Joon Chang's, *Kicking Away the Ladder*

David Graeber's, *Debt: The First 5000 Years*

Robert E. Lucas's, *Why Doesn't Capital Flow from Rich To Poor Countries?*

Thomas Piketty's, *Capital in the Twenty-First Century*

Amartya Sen's, *Inequality Re-Examined*

Mahbub Ul Haq's, *Reflections on Human Development*

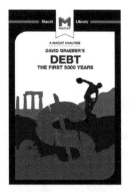
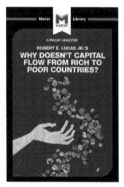

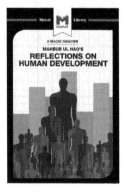

Macat analyses are available from all good bookshops and libraries.

Access hundreds of analyses through one, multimedia tool.
Join free for one month **library.macat.com**

Macat Disciplines

Access the greatest ideas and thinkers across entire disciplines, including

GLOBALIZATION

Arjun Appadurai's, *Modernity at Large: Cultural Dimensions of Globalisation*

James Ferguson's, *The Anti-Politics Machine*

Geert Hofstede's, *Culture's Consequences*

Amartya Sen's, *Development as Freedom*

Macat Pairs

Analyse historical and modern issues from opposite sides of an argument. Pairs include:

HOW TO RUN AN ECONOMY

John Maynard Keynes's
The General Theory OF Employment, Interest and Money

Classical economics suggests that market economies are self-correcting in times of recession or depression, and tend toward full employment and output. But English economist John Maynard Keynes disagrees.

In his ground-breaking 1936 study *The General Theory*, Keynes argues that traditional economics has misunderstood the causes of unemployment. Employment is not determined by the price of labor; it is directly linked to demand. Keynes believes market economies are by nature unstable, and so require government intervention. Spurred on by the social catastrophe of the Great Depression of the 1930s, he sets out to revolutionize the way the world thinks

Milton Friedman's
The Role of Monetary Policy

Friedman's 1968 paper changed the course of economic theory. In just 17 pages, he demolished existing theory and outlined an effective alternate monetary policy designed to secure 'high employment, stable prices and rapid growth.'

Friedman demonstrated that monetary policy plays a vital role in broader economic stability and argued that economists got their monetary policy wrong in the 1950s and 1960s by misunderstanding the relationship between inflation and unemployment. Previous generations of economists had believed that governments could permanently decrease unemployment by permitting inflation—and vice versa. Friedman's most original contribution was to show that this supposed trade-off is an illusion that only works in the short term.

Macat analyses are available from all good bookshops and libraries.

Access hundreds of analyses through one, multimedia tool.
Join free for one month **library.macat.com**

Macat Disciplines

Access the greatest ideas and thinkers across entire disciplines, including

THE FUTURE OF DEMOCRACY

Robert A. Dahl's, *Democracy and Its Critics*
Robert A. Dahl's, *Who Governs?*
Alexis De Toqueville's, *Democracy in America*
Niccolò Machiavelli's, *The Prince*
John Stuart Mill's, *On Liberty*
Robert D. Putnam's, *Bowling Alone*
Jean-Jacques Rousseau's, *The Social Contract*
Henry David Thoreau's, *Civil Disobedience*

Macat Disciplines

Access the greatest ideas and thinkers across entire disciplines, including

TOTALITARIANISM

Sheila Fitzpatrick's, *Everyday Stalinism*
Ian Kershaw's, *The "Hitler Myth"*
Timothy Snyder's, *Bloodlands*

Macat Pairs

Analyse historical and modern issues from opposite sides of an argument. Pairs include:

RACE AND IDENTITY

Zora Neale Hurston's
Characteristics of Negro Expression

Using material collected on anthropological expeditions to the South, Zora Neale Hurston explains how expression in African American culture in the early twentieth century departs from the art of white America. At the time, African American art was often criticized for copying white culture. For Hurston, this criticism misunderstood how art works. European tradition views art as something fixed. But Hurston describes a creative process that is alive, ever-changing, and largely improvisational. She maintains that African American art works through a process called 'mimicry'—where an imitated object or verbal pattern, for example, is reshaped and altered until it becomes something new, novel—and worthy of attention.

Frantz Fanon's
Black Skin, White Masks

Black Skin, White Masks offers a radical analysis of the psychological effects of colonization on the colonized.

Fanon witnessed the effects of colonization first hand both in his birthplace, Martinique, and again later in life when he worked as a psychiatrist in another French colony, Algeria. His text is uncompromising in form and argument. He dissects the dehumanizing effects of colonialism, arguing that it destroys the native sense of identity, forcing people to adapt to an alien set of values—including a core belief that they are inferior. This results in deep psychological trauma.

Fanon's work played a pivotal role in the civil rights movements of the 1960s.

Macat analyses are available from all good bookshops and libraries.

Access hundreds of analyses through one, multimedia tool.
Join free for one month **library.macat.com**

Printed in the United States
by Baker & Taylor Publisher Services